CICO BOOKS
LONDON NEW YORK

ROMANTIC
IRISH HOMES

ROBERT O'BYRNE

photography by **SIMON BROWN**

This edition published in 2013 by CICO Books

First published in 2009 by CICO Books
An imprint of Ryland Peters & Small
20–21 Jockey's Fields   519 Broadway, 5th Floor
London WC1R 4BW   New York, NY 10012

10 9 8 7 6 5 4 3 2 1

A CIP catalog record for this book is available from the
Library of Congress and the British Library.

ISBN: 978 1 908862 90 7

Printed in China

Editor: Gillian Haslam
Designer: Paul Tilby
Photographer: Simon Brown

CONTENTS

INTRODUCTION

OPPOSITE: In a corner of the library at Tullynally, County Westmeath, a door opens into a turret.

ABOVE, FROM LEFT TO RIGHT: A view of Ken and Rachel Thompson's home in County Cork; a candelabra in the dining room of Mari Saville's house outside Letterfrack, County Galway; and the bell pull of Higginsbrook, County Meath.

BELOW: The old postbox at Higginsbrook remains in service.

What is it that gives the Irish house such a distinctive character? After all, in theory these buildings should look no different from those found on the neighboring island of Britain and yet the Irish house is quite different in appearance and spirit. Why should this be so? Why should the houses of Ireland appear quite unlike those found on the other side of a short stretch of water?

Perhaps water itself holds at least a part-explanation. Ireland is a notoriously wet country, one in which rain is an almost-daily occurrence. The climate is cold and damp, the air always heavy with moisture. While this keeps the fields green, it also leaves the skies gray. For centuries Irish landscape painting has been full of scudding clouds that dominate a low horizon; in fact, these canvases usually feature more sky than land which is represented by a thin spit of color in the foreground. Sunlight is something of a rarity in Ireland, the cause of national excitement when it does occur. But more often the daily forecast is for rain in abundance, and in response the Irish fall back on euphemism when speaking of the weather. A "soft day," for example, is one during which persistent but not necessarily drenching rain falls, while a heavier downpour is frequently excused with the remark that "the farmers will be glad of it."

But the truth is that gray sometimes seems to be the national color—not for nothing did one of the last century's most famous poets, Patrick Kavanagh, write of the "stony grey soil of Monaghan," his native county. The sky is gray, the earth

OPPOSITE: In an early Georgian house on Dublin's Henrietta Street, the walls have been left unaltered by the present owner to display the accretions of centuries.

TOP: A model of Mount Rivers, County Cork sits on top of an old piano in the house's morning room.

ABOVE: Old paper and faded curtains in a bedroom of Stradbally Hall, County Laois.

is gray, the stone is gray; even the mood of the people can be similarly shaded. So no wonder that when it comes to their homes, the Irish respond to all that grayness by embracing color in a way that might elsewhere seem reckless but here makes sense. And it makes sense because the native palette is nothing like that seen elsewhere. The Irish do not embrace the candy colors of the Mediterranean; bright pinks and tones of turquoise and lavender are not, as a rule, found in their homes. Nor do they opt for the cool neutrals preferred by the Scandinavians, those bleached shades of pale blue and lilac.

Instead, the Irish taste is for colors that are strong, sometimes primary, sometimes surprisingly dark. It might be thought, for instance, that given the gray air outdoors, dark red or green would be spurned for interiors. But on the contrary, they are embraced because it has been understood that these colors come alive in artificial light, a great deal of which is needed given the Irish climate. A room with deep crimson walls is commonplace in Ireland, as is the use of yellow in every conceivable variety from canary to ocher. Yellow, in fact, works especially well as a counterbalance to gray skies; it brings warmth and cheer into any house, especially when appreciated by the glow of an open fire. Although some recently-built homes have large expanses of glass, the windows of Irish houses were traditionally small, designed to admit whatever light was necessary but also to minimize awareness of the gloomy weather outside. So without the bold use of color, rooms can be dark and unappealing. Similarly white, which might seem an obvious solution, can sometimes work in very large spaces but where smaller rooms are concerned it is too hard and only accentuates the chill of an average Irish day. In Ireland color provides heat even before the fire is lit.

The damp of the local climate helps to explain the general preference in Ireland for paint over wallpaper. Though the latter is found in some houses, it has to contend with the constant threat of peeling. Not that a little shabbiness is shunned in Ireland. On the contrary, long before it became fashionable elsewhere, shabby chic was a norm among the Irish simply because for many years there was no other option; the country's relative poverty meant owners had to live with their old furniture and decoration no matter how

worn it had become. Although Ireland underwent an economic resurgence from the mid-1990s onward, there are still plenty of houses around the country which, despite their architectural splendors, still hold curtains that will shred if tugged too aggressively and carpets so worn that the floorboards beneath can be inspected. In some cases this is because the owners did not benefit from the boom, but in others it is due to an appreciation of the items' inherent qualities, the gentle sheen that only age and use can give to an object.

Hence the fondness for old pieces of furniture like the Irish mahogany hunting table, a staple in so many Irish houses. With its two drop leaves, over the centuries the hunting table has performed a multitude of functions from accommodating a large dinner group to supporting the coffin during a wake. Ideally it should not look too shiny or smart; the best furniture wears its accumulated history with pride and the occasional scratch or chip should be the cause of no shame. At the same time, it is perfectly permissible to mix the old with the new, rather in the way that, in the pre-boom years, portraits of the Pope and President John Kennedy hung side by side on the parlor wall of Catholic homesteads and both were equally reverenced. Likewise, even contemporary Irish homes will contain a blend of the antique and the modern, the heirlooms and the latest acquisitions.

The recent advent of economic prosperity has brought many changes to Ireland, not least to the living standards of her citizens, many of whom within living memory had to make do with very poor quality housing. Although a lot of the country's new homes have less overt charm than their antecedents, they provide their occupants with more comfort than was formerly the case: a thatched Irish cottage may look appealing but its interior is usually dark and dank. Under these circumstances, the appeal of a well-insulated and bright bungalow can be understood. In the popular imagination, an old house is associated with the old times when there was little money and a lot of hardship. A new building, on the other hand, is symbolic of the improvement enjoyed by the entire nation and hence its appeal. Nevertheless, despite all the changes, there remain plenty of houses throughout the country which still retain their original distinctive character, the same one that has always made the Irish home unlike that found anywhere else.

OPPOSITE: The present occupant of Mount Rivers is an inveterate collector, especially of family memorabilia as this corner of the drawing room reveals.

TOP: An array of portrait miniatures hung on the wall of a guest bedroom at Tullynally.

ABOVE: A small chest of drawers stands against the roughly white-washed walls of a bedroom in Castle Dodard, County Waterford.

FARMHOUSES

THE POPULAR IMAGE OF THE IRISH FARMHOUSE HAS LONG BEEN FIXED IN THE GLOBAL MIND. INVARIABLY CONSISTING OF JUST ONE STOREY, IT HAS WHITE-WASHED WALLS AND A THATCHED ROOF, AS WELL AS AN EQUALLY SIMPLE, MUD-FLOORED INTERIOR IN WHICH A TURF FIRE IS FOREVER SMOKING. FEW SUCH HOUSES EXIST ANYMORE AND NO WONDER, FOR THEY WERE DANK, MISERABLE PLACES THAT BRED ILL-HEALTH AND UNHAPPINESS. FORTUNATELY A GOOD NUMBER OF LARGER, BETTER-CONSTRUCTED FARMHOUSES HAVE SURVIVED, ALTHOUGH OFTEN ABANDONED AND IN A POOR STATE OF REPAIR. OF LATE, HOWEVER, MANY SUCH DWELLINGS HAVE BEEN CAREFULLY RESTORED TO PROVIDE EITHER PERMANENT OR HOLIDAY HOMES FOR THOSE WITH ENOUGH IMAGINATION TO RECOGNIZE THEIR CHARM AND POTENTIAL.

RIGHT AND FAR RIGHT: The only substantial alteration made to this property by its present owner was the alteration of the façade where three glazed double doors were inserted and a deep limestone terrace created immediately beyond. From this spot, perfect for pre-lunch and dinner drinks, there are outstanding views across the lawn and through a copse of mature trees to a coastline of seemingly endless alternating headlands and coves. During the summer, the owner often descends to the nearest shoreline to swim.

THE "STRONG FARMERS" HOUSE
COUNTY CORK

In the popular imagination, rural Ireland holds only two kinds of domestic dwelling: the Big House occupied by members of the gentry and aristocracy and, right at the other end of the scale, the thatched cottage which provided shelter for the majority of the population. True, for many centuries these were the country's dominant vernacular architectural models, but they were never the only ones. In particular, it is a mistake to imagine that everyone not living in a castle or Palladian mansion had the sole alternative of a small white-washed cottage. In fact, from the eighteenth century onward substantial, two-storey houses were constructed by and for "Strong Farmers," a social group perhaps unique to Ireland.

OPPOSITE: The house's contents are described by its owner as being "nothing particularly valuable, just little vernacular pieces." Nevertheless, they have been selected with care, as can be seen by the carved oak and rattan armchair in the living room. Behind it stands a nineteenth-century oak table in the manner of Pugin. On the wall above hangs a seascape inherited from an aunt who was inclined to embellish the pictures she owned, in this instance by adding a hay scene to one side of the canvas.

Until the early 1900s, when legal reforms allowed large-scale transference of property to take place, the greater part of the country was owned by a relatively small number of landlords who leased much of their agricultural holdings to tenant farmers. Most of the latter could afford to rent only tiny parcels of land; prior to the onset of the Great Famine in 1845, almost half the population somehow managed to support their families on ten acres or often much less. This was the class most vulnerable to any economic or agricultural setback, and therefore most affected by the failure of the

potato crop over several successive years during the second half of the 1840s. It was also the group most likely to be found occupying the traditional white-washed and thatched cottage. The Irish Strong Farmer, on the other hand, might rent up to several hundred acres from an aristocratic landlord and usually did so on a much longer lease than those offered to smallholders. Although no more than 15 percent of the pre-Famine population could be classified as Strong Farmers, nevertheless this caste rented the great bulk of Irish land, often subletting it to the less affluent. Security of tenure combined with a decent income allowed these wealthier farmers to carry out improvements on their land, not least the construction of sturdy buildings. As historian Kerby Miller has noted of the period, traditionally the houses of Strong Farmers were "well-built—perhaps two-storied, with stone walls and roofs which were slated rather than thatched—and well furnished."

Such is very much the case with the farmhouse seen here. Although dating from the late nineteenth/early twentieth century, it is of a style that had remained relatively unaltered over the previous 100 years. Located

in a remote corner of the south-east of the country, the house originally lay at the center of a 100-acre holding. Before the advent of electricity, telephones, and especially motor transport, it must have been an isolated spot and even now the house is not easy to find, discovered at the end of increasingly minor roads which eventually dwindle into a narrow boreen—the Irish term for a rough, unsurfaced country track. Today the isolation gives the place a romantic appeal, as do the surrounding vistas of rolling fields on three sides of the property—the fourth offers an uninterrupted view of the Irish Sea several hundred feet below; during the summer months, the house's present owner often descends to the shore for a swim.

When he first came across the building in 2004, it had been unoccupied for more than

ABOVE: An oak table in the drawing room is covered in bowls bought in Bulgaria. Beyond hang two paintings by Irish artist Kathy Prendergast.

OPPOSITE: Gathered around an Irish mahogany drop-leaf hunting table in the living room is an assortment of oak chairs. Like much of the house's contents, the button-back leather armchair was an antique shop find.

Strong Farmers' homes were never known for their decoration
and this example has a typically unpretentious simplicity.

OPPOSITE AND ABOVE: The kitchen
has been left almost untouched,
other than the addition of some
tongue-and-groove cupboards.
Otherwise the mottled ocher walls
retain their original paint, the quarry
tiles on the floor are still in place,
and the shelving is unaltered.

half a century since the death of a previous occupant. No doubt the
remoteness of the setting had discouraged anybody else from settling
there, as did the plainness of the house: Strong Farmers' homes were never
known for their decorative detail and this particular example possesses
an unpretentious simplicity typical of the genus. Wisely the new owner
has not attempted to conceal the plainness, but instead saw the house
as an opportunity to celebrate the virtues of clean, unfussy design. First,
however, he had to undertake a program of basic restoration since at
the time of purchase the building was close to collapse. The roof needed
attention, as did the walls, doors, and windows. Internally the main
feature to be salvaged was the staircase, although even that needed
repair and replacement in sections.

During this work, changes were made to the south, sea-facing front,
with the three existing windows lowered to create a trio of double doors

LEFT, RIGHT, AND OPPOSITE: The owner intended to make this room into his new kitchen and installed an Aga oven for that purpose. But then he came across the painted dresser, now replete with examples of highly collectible early Irish spongeware and Belleek pottery, and so decided to change his plans. Now it acts as a dining room with pine table and chairs occupying the greater part of the space and the old oven serving as a fireplace on cold nights. The framed maritime map behind the Belfast sink shows the local section of the Irish coast.

A low-key decorative approach has been adopted by the owner, with clay plaster used to cover the walls of the dining room, which is furnished in plain pine.

opening onto a terrace flagged with limestone; when weather permits, this area is used for entertaining. In addition the first-floor plate-glass windows were changed to double sashes with glazing bars, a modification which immediately softened the house's unadorned severity. As was always the custom with these properties, the exterior walls of stone are cement-rendered and then left without even a lime wash. Several out-buildings have also been restored, a vegetable garden created, and a secure area for hens devised. Otherwise, the rest of the 20 acres acquired by the owner has been left in its familiar state of fields interspersed with copses of trees.

The same low-key approach has been adopted inside the house. The kitchen, for example, retains its original tiled floor and as much of the old ocher and red wall coloring as could be preserved; new cupboards have been sympathetically painted to harmonize with what was already in situ. The dining room opposite is equally understated, with clay plaster used to cover the walls and the furnishings in plain pine. A slightly more elaborate approach was taken to the decoration

OPPOSITE TOP LEFT: On a shelf above the bed in the main suite rest a variety of bibelots, including several pieces of contemporary Irish pottery and a seventeenth-century Indian sculpture. On the left-hand side can be seen a traditional Irish painted pine settle bed, which folds up during the day to become a seat.

OPPOSITE TOP RIGHT: A pair of ancient Irish elk horns rest on an oak Gothic revival table in the master bedroom. The blue glaze bowl beneath is Spanish.

LEFT: A pair of old ceramic floor tiles found by the owner rest on top of the bedhead in the main guest bedroom.

OPPOSITE BOTTOM LEFT: To accommodate the occasional overflow of guests, the owner installed bunk beds in one of the upper rooms.

OPPOSITE BOTTOM RIGHT: In the owner's bedroom, the space between two windows is filled by an old Irish vernacular cabinet such as would once have been found in many houses like this.

Intended as a weekend retreat, the house exudes comfort and ease.

of the two reception rooms to the front of the house but they share the same comfortable, unassuming character found elsewhere. Chairs, tables, and other pieces of furniture were picked up over a period of time, says their owner, none of them for a great price. Most of the pictures were acquired in the same way or were painted by friends.

Not a full-time home, the property is intended as a retreat and tends to be most often visited at weekends when friends are invited over for lunches and dinners. Although no longer owned by a Strong Farmer, it is clear this house continues to inspire a strong affection.

OPPOSITE: The drawing room is furnished with an idiosyncratic mixture of the old and the new, the bought and the salvaged. Above the fireplace hangs an abstract oil by an unknown artist bought at an auction in the Irish midlands, while to its right is a small canvas depicting St Patrick banishing the snakes from Ireland.

RIGHT AND FAR RIGHT: To the rear of the house the owner has created a series of gardens based around outbuildings, some of which have been restored while others offer a romantic prospect from the owner's terrace leading to an allée of hornbeams. The sculpture of a deer was made from pieces of found wood.

THE FARMHOUSE
COUNTY CORK

The Palladian house model first introduced to Ireland in the early eighteenth century quickly became popular throughout the country and while originally intended for homes of the aristocracy, it was adapted to suit the domestic requirements of all levels of society.

W ithin a century the design of even the humblest Irish farmhouse might contain echoes of its grander neighbors. In particular, the formal arrangement of outbuildings such as barns, sheds, and byres around the main residence was very much in the classical manner. These additional structures were placed either to each side of a forecourt before the front door or else positioned in a similar fashion to the rear.

The second layout is seen at the farmhouse shown here, an archetype of the genre in its functionality and absence of unnecessary decoration. It is impossible to date the building, since stylistically it could have been erected at any point between the late eighteenth and mid-twentieth centuries. As Dublin architects Niall McCullough and Valerie Mulvin observe in their 1987 book *A Lost Tradition: The Nature of Architecture*

ABOVE: Irish farmhouses were traditionally simple dwellings with no effort made to discuss their essentially utilitarian purpose. The owner has wisely decided not to disguise his home's origins but has preserved its modest exterior features.

in Ireland, "The tradition of these plain houses without detail somehow survived the eclectic games of the Victorian age..." From the start, they conformed to certain norms in all having the same thick walls made from rubble stone covered in render as well as small, almost square, windows and single pitch roofs covered in heavy slate.

Inside they were equally understated, with a narrow entrance hall leading to the best room, or parlor on the left (a room rarely used except on special occasions such as a visit from the parish priest) while to the right stood the family room and kitchen. A staircase

It takes a particular eye to recognize the traditional Irish farmhouse's special merits.

would lead to several bedrooms on the first floor. The starkness of these houses' design led to their fall from favor in recent decades as Ireland grew more affluent and farming families sought a greater degree of comfort. Throughout the country large numbers of old farmhouses were simply abandoned in favor of new bungalows and the majority of them fell into complete ruin. It takes a particular eye to recognize the merits of this housing type and fortunately the owner of the house in question possesses just such an eye.

When he first saw his home 12 years ago, it had been unoccupied for more than two

ABOVE LEFT: The work unit in the center of the kitchen took its form and design from a long, shallow mahogany cabinet originally made for a pharmacy in the Irish midlands.

ABOVE RIGHT: The kitchen chimney has been preserved and is now used for heating the room and on occasions also for cooking.

LEFT: An old wooden box found in one of the outbuildings has been used to display ceramics bought from a student show in Cork.

OPPOSITE: The dresser is a fine example of these once-common pieces of traditional farmhouse kitchen furniture. Now highly collectible, such impressive pieces are at the core of the home, providing a focal point for displaying ceramics of all kinds. Here, the pieces of contemporary pottery by John ffrench are shown off to full advantage.

decades and, as he says, "the place was in rag order." Cattle had gained access to the ground floor which as a result had turned into a mess of churned mud. Neither plumbing nor electrical wiring had ever been installed and most of the windows were missing. Thankfully the slate roof had somehow survived, but even so the restoration program took some 12 months, with the owner acting as his own architect. Four years ago he embarked on further building work to add a large kitchen at the back of the house, constructing it on the footprint of an old outbuilding.

At all stages, while comforts such as bathrooms were added, the owner wisely never attempted to disguise his home's relatively humble origins. So, for example, the original tongue-and-groove paneled ceilings have been retained. Likewise in the kitchen/dining areas, the floor is covered in nothing grander than

untreated concrete tiles, albeit they enjoy the benefit of underfloor heating; elsewhere plain seagrass matting has been used. On the first floor, the old doors and their surrounds were kept intact since these had been carefully "grained" by a previous occupant to give the impression that they were made from expensive dark wood rather than cheap pine.

And former residents would have appreciated some of the present furniture, such as the stained kitchen table surrounded by dark green chairs; timber was often painted in Irish farmhouses both to disguise the fact that different woods had been used in the same piece and to provide some very necessary color. That was certainly the case with the large painted dresser dominating the kitchen. Once a staple in every Irish farmhouse, thousands of these pieces were thrown out of homes in the closing decades of the last century and whatever survives is now highly collectible. This example, with its paneled doors and carved board, is especially fine and acts as an ideal display unit for some of the owner's substantial collection of John ffrench pottery. Raised in his family home, Castle

ffrench in County Galway (which was noted for its exuberant plasterwork featuring birds, leaves, and flowers), this pioneering Irish modernist has been working as a ceramicist since the early 1950s and examples of his work across the past half-century can be found throughout the farmhouse.

OPPOSITE AND BELOW: In the dining room, a cloth-covered sideboard holds part of a large Mason ironware service beneath a photograph by artist Gary Coyle. The Victorian mahogany table and sideboard were picked up at auction and provide an effective counterpoint to the floor of untreated concrete tiles.

BELOW LEFT: A view through the house, looking from the dining room via the hall to the drawing room and the library beyond.

So too can pictures by young Irish artists, such as Gary Coyle and Ciaran O Cearnaigh. But the house holds older artwork too, not least an unsigned Cubist abstract in the drawing room, which also contains a small, quirky oil depicting St Patrick banishing the snakes from Ireland. Bought for just a few pounds from an antique dealer in Cork city, this is the item the owner says he would first rescue in the unhappy event of a fire. The confident mixture of old and new is evident in every room, not least the kitchen where a glass-fronted nineteenth-century mahogany display cabinet, originally made for a pharmacy, has been incorporated into a modern work unit. Similarly, in the owner's bedroom a stripped pine table once belonging to his mother stands beneath a large picture by Irish abstract artist Paul Mosse. Different cultures also comfortably exist alongside each other. On one wall in the drawing room hangs a framed piece of antique woven cloth from Laos, while the small library is filled with fabrics from Morocco.

A confident mixture of the old and the new is evident in every room.

A keen chef, the owner has paid as much attention to the grounds of his home as to its interior. He has created a new vegetable garden and last year planted an orchard containing 40 different trees: apple, pear, quince, medlar, and damson. He already keeps chickens and having been given a hive, the next project is to produce his own honey. Seemingly destined to become a ruin like so many of its ilk, this old Irish farmhouse has been returned to vibrant life.

OPPOSITE: A plinth of untreated wood supports another of John ffrench's distinctive ceramics, bought from the back of a car. The large canvas beyond the mahogany drop-leaf hunting table is by painter Ciaran O Cearnaigh.

ABOVE: The guest bedroom is home to a variety of pictures, including watercolors by the owner's late mother and these racing prints.

BALLYTRASNA
COUNTY CORK

County Cork is a part of Ireland that has always attracted creative spirits, many of whom find inspiration in the scenic coastal region lying to the west of Cork city. For some reason its eastern equivalent, although equally attractive, has never proven as popular, but Ken and Rachel Thompson are one couple who have long appreciated its appeal.

OPPOSITE: Now one large space designed to serve a wide variety of purposes, when first bought by Ken and Rachel Thompson the main part of the old cottage was divided into seven rooms.

ABOVE LEFT AND RIGHT: Although close to the sea, the house and its outbuildings nestle in a hollow that provides shelter and allows the Thompsons to grow much of their own produce.

Ken comes from an old merchant family which for a century and a half, from 1835 onward, owned the well-known Cork bakery F H Thompson & Sons Ltd. A highly spiritual man, at the end of his schooling he considered becoming a Benedictine monk but put aside the idea when his older brother entered Downside Abbey as a novice; Ken felt it would be unfair on his parents to lose two sons to the church. Instead, he spent two years training as a master baker in London followed by the same amount of time again learning the art of chocolate-making in Belgium and Germany. Then, during a short spell in Liverpool, he discovered his true vocation while watching stonemasons at work on the west front of Gilbert Scott's Anglican cathedral.

Since that time Ken Thompson has become one of Ireland's most renowned sculptors, with examples of his work found not only throughout the country but further afield. His "Memorial to Innocent Victims" stands just outside the west door of Westminster Abbey, while not far away in Westminster Cathedral he was responsible for the monument to the late Cardinal Basil Hume.

Ken Thompson's exceptional abilities were immediately recognized, not least by Joan and Rene Hague, daughter and son-in-law of the English sculptor, typographer, and wood engraver Eric Gill. Together with their

Until acquired by its present owners, the house had been occupied
by a farmer who refused all previous offers to buy the place.

ABOVE LEFT: The Thompsons'
preference for simple, unadorned
materials is evident in the extensive
use of tongue-and-groove paneling.

ABOVE RIGHT: Carved by Ken
Thompson, the stone lintel at the
end of this corridor bears the words
"migraturus habita", which translate
as "Dwell as if about to depart."

OPPOSITE: The house's original
large fireplace was discovered buried
beneath centuries' old accretions and
would once have been used to cook
the occupants' food.

daughter, they had settled in East Cork not far from the spot where Ken
and Rachel, a painter born in England, would eventually come to live.
Rene Hague gave Ken his very first commission, for a small marble trough
carved with an inscription. In the meantime, Ken and Rachel, who were
newly married, spent a couple of years in Italy.

On their return to Ireland they and their growing family settled in an
eighteenth-century stable block in the grounds of his parents' home at
Carrigtwohill, County Cork and although they were very happy there, the
couple always spent a certain amount of time in East Cork which Ken had
known from his childhood when his maternal grandmother owned a hotel
in the fishing port of Ballycotton. It was while walking in the area one wet
January day in 1990 that they found their present home, which at the
time they thought was a ruin; on inspection it turned out to be occupied

by a local farmer who had resisted all previous offers to buy the place. "But the day after we met," recalls Ken, "he rang me up and said he'd sell the house to us." Given that they had succeeded where everybody else had failed, the Thompsons felt they had to acquire the house despite the fact that it was completely dilapidated and scarcely habitable. Though tucked away in a hollow and therefore sheltered from the strong winds that sweep across this part of the coast, the building had received little attention from its previous occupants and required a complete overhaul.

Although the precise date of the house's original construction cannot be confirmed, it must date back at least 200 years and is possibly even older.

Almost all the work of restoration was undertaken by Ken, not least the creation of what is today the couple's main kitchen/living room. At the time of its purchase this space was divided into seven rooms and had to be totally gutted. "We took the roof off and raised the level by about a foot before re-covering it with old slates." Quite at what date the house was first constructed is impossible to discover, but it must date back at least 200 years. The present substantial fireplace, for example, was buried beneath layers of board and plaster that were gradually removed "until we got right back and found the original opening with

OPPOSITE: Despite the fact that they left interiors in semi-gloom, the windows in Irish houses tended to be small and set deep within thick walls because of the need to preserve as much heat as possible in a cold and damp climate.

ABOVE: Plate racks such as that seen here were once a feature of every Irish farmhouse, but like so much other traditional country furniture they have almost vanished from today's homes.

Over the past thirty years, Ken Thompson has become
one of Ireland's most renowned sculptors, his work
being found throughout the country.

ABOVE AND RIGHT: Ken
Thompson's studio stands directly
opposite the original farmhouse and
below the main bedroom, allowing
him to integrate his work into his
everyday life.

OPPOSITE: Though originally
expected to work in the family
bakery business, while still in his
early twenties Ken found his true
vocation which was to be a sculptor,
a career in which he has enjoyed
success ever since.

its blackened beam." Initially the Thompsons
intended to use the house only as a holiday
home and just bought the land immediately
around the building. However, they found
themselves spending more and more time
there and in 1997 moved permanently, having
acquired several more acres and planted
hundreds of trees and other vegetation in
order to ensure their long-term privacy.
During this time they carried out additional
work on the building and its outhouses
which now wrap around an almost enclosed

courtyard. Off the kitchen section of the main house's great room, they added a wing that holds a small sitting room, bedroom, and bathroom. At its end lies the entrance to what was once a barn, the upper storeys now given over to additional bedrooms and a studio, while below are two workshops where Ken works. As an expression of his strong religious faith, he converted a small building on the fourth side of the "courtyard" into a chapel, its plain white-washed interior holding a stained glass panel by Irish artist Patrick Pye and a primitive seventeenth-century Dutch crucifix. The complex of buildings with their different roof heights has been so snugly fitted into the folds of the landscape that it is invisible from the road.

A similar reticence is apparent indoors. The Thompson home is decorated without fuss or ostentation and using natural materials as much as possible. Many of the floors are covered in limestone flags while ceilings are

The Thompsons' home is decorated without fuss
or any kind of ostentation, and the couple has
tried to use natural materials as much as possible.

of unpainted wood, as is much of the furniture while handwoven fabrics
abound, hanging as curtains or thrown over sofas and chairs. A stone lintel
at the end of a long corridor in the house has been carved with the Latin
words *migraturus habita*: "dwell as if about to depart." Though the house
has become both their home and place of work, the Thompsons know
nothing is permanent. "This place is not in any way detached from my art,"
observes Ken. "Moving here, I was trying to find a way of life that would
have some kind of integrity."

OPPOSITE: Perhaps reflecting Ken
Thompson's adolescent ambitions to
join a religious order, the interior of
his home has a monastic simplicity
and is devoid of superfluous
decoration. Roughly-rendered walls
have been white washed, woodwork
left unvarnished or painted, and
floors covered in sisal.

ABOVE: The Thompsons' bedroom
shares the same spirit of purity and
understatement found elsewhere in
the house.

OPPOSITE: Flagged in tiles that came from a local quarry, this large room was always the heart of the house. The open fireplace, which now holds a wood-burning stove, would have been kept going at all times, both to provide heating and for cooking purposes. The old beams are original to the house.

RIGHT AND FAR RIGHT: Whereas many farmhouses in Ireland are gable-ended, this one has a hipped roof, an indication of its original owner's relative wealth. The house always stood behind a low stone wall facing onto a gravel courtyard around which the other farm buildings were sited.

BELOW: The ironwork gates are now some two centuries old and still fine, as are the slates that cover both the main house and all its outbuildings.

TIPPERARY FARMHOUSE
COUNTY TIPPERARY

Because Ireland's Great Famine of 1845–48 had such devastating and long-term consequences, not least the death of approximately one million of the native population, it is often forgotten how prosperous the country was prior to this catastrophe. During the early decades of the nineteenth century, Ireland's economy was predominantly agricultural and as a result the island was able not only to feed all its own inhabitants (numbering some eight million immediately prior to the years of famine), but also to be a net exporter of food.

Large parts of the country enjoyed unprecedented prosperity, not least South Tipperary where the land is some of the most fertile in Ireland. Thanks to this affluence, there was something of a rural building boom in the post-1800 period with many new homes constructed for both landowners and their more successful tenants. The South Tipperary house shown here would appear to be just such a property. Standing on land that was once part of a very large estate, it was probably built by and for a lessee at the very start of the nineteenth century; the wide overhanging

eaves are very much a feature of that period and in this instance they project almost a foot from the walls, supported on slabs of cantilevered slate. The same slate, which comes from a local quarry that was extensively mined in earlier centuries but has long since been abandoned, also covers the roof which is hipped rather than gable-nded. The latter style, easier and less expensive to create, is the norm across much of Ireland and hipped roofs tend to be found in those parts of the countryside where farmers enjoyed the largest incomes. In this instance, the roof was so well constructed that when the present owner bought the house in 1995, he found it required no restoration other than replacement of old guttering.

On the other hand, a lot of work had to be done to the interior because, even though uninterruptedly occupied from the time of its construction until the late 1980s, the house had no plumbing of any kind and the only evidence of electricity was a single light bulb hanging from the ceiling in the original kitchen, parlor, and principal bedroom. The last of these rooms contained souvenirs of the building's previous occupant: side by side on a wall hung photographs of the local elected parliamentary representative and the Pope.

Throughout the premises, the new owner found indications that the original builders had aspirations to raise themselves in the social hierarchy of pre-famine Ireland. "It's quite primitive in design in certain areas," he remarks, "and quite sophisticated in others—almost as if it's bi-polar." The most obviously primitive aspect of the house's design is found in its treatment of the staircase which, in spite of its elegant joinery, is awkwardly sited to cut across the frame of a door leading into a former pantry (now the kitchen). Likewise, its wide treads interrupt the lines of the window immediately beyond. These unsatisfactorily resolved design issues suggest the house's first owners wanted to build themselves a home that aped aspects of bigger properties

OPPOSITE AND THIS PAGE: The parlor was unquestionably the best room in a house of this kind, and not necessarily used on a daily basis. The aspirations of earlier owners can be seen in such details as the pine flooring, the cornice running around the top of the walls, and the elegant corner cabinet in which the best pieces of family china would have been stored. The present owner has furnished the room with a mixture of inherited pieces and items picked up inexpensively at auction or bought on his travels.

"It's quite primitive in design in some areas," says the owner, "and sophisticated in others."

OPPOSITE: The main room continues to act as the house's key space since all other rooms are accessed from here. It is dominated by a table made by furniture maker Clive Nunn of Thomastown, County Kilkenny and a set of chairs by Eric Conor. To the rear are two doors leading to what were once the pantry and perhaps a maid's room, now a kitchen and bathroom.

TOP LEFT: As if to emphasize the fact that the strictly functional main room held quite a different status to the parlor, the two are separated by this small, paneled corridor.

TOP RIGHT: One of the most important jobs was preserving as much of the old windows as possible. Each was dismantled and examined, and only wood and glass that absolutely had to be replaced were so. "There isn't a single window that isn't at least fifty percent of the original," says the owner.

but obviously were not sufficiently wealthy or important enough to employ an architect or able to work out certain technical difficulties for themselves.

On the other hand, they were in a position to borrow certain decorative details from elsewhere and to impose these on the structure. The space above the main bedroom's windows, for example, is filled with curved plaster ornamentation that makes the room look far grander than would otherwise be the case. And in the parlor immediately below, a handsome, glass-fronted cabinet was inserted into the wall to the immediate left of the fireplace, presumably for the display of cherished pieces of china and other heirlooms. All the windows have the same fine shutters (and, like the window frames, these were taken out during the period of restoration and repaired) but on the ground floor metal bars protect the windows from possible intruders—another sign of the early tenant farmers' relative prosperity.

What the present owner describes as the house's "bi-polar" character can be found also in the different ceiling treatments: those in the parlor and main bedroom are plastered and corniced (and had center plaster roses—although no light ever hung from either), whereas that in the central room—which would once have been the kitchen—has exposed

OPPOSITE AND THIS PAGE: To one side of the courtyard in front of the farmhouse stands a small building, one part of which served as a calf house while the other was a hen house. Seeking to preserve the severely dilapidated structure and to provide additional guest accommodation, the present owner opened up the interior and created a self-contained unit. In the living/sleeping area, the exposed stone walls feature niches where hens would have sat while laying their eggs.

beams and, in contrast to the parlor's elegant fitted cabinet, contained a traditional dresser, the impression of which could still be seen on one wall when the present owner bought the house. Likewise, instead of plaster, the big upper landing ceiling was originally open to the rafters but for a long time has been covered in painted timber sheeting. This first-floor landing is one of the house's most distinctive attributes. Located directly above the kitchen which had a big open fireplace, it would most likely have been warmer than the bedrooms to either side and so perhaps this was where the house's children slept.

Outdoors a more pragmatic approach was taken by the property's builders, with various farm structures like barn, piggery, hen house, and cattle sheds grouped around two further sides of a graveled courtyard. The fourth side is occupied by an entrance wall and handsome cast-iron gates which must be now some 200 years old. The neighboring calf and hen houses have been re-roofed and opened up to create a convenient, self-contained guest cottage for visitors. Because this space was entirely functional and in such poor condition, the present owner quite rightly adopted a more contemporary approach to its design, splitting the interior into two sections separated by a central box containing a bathroom. Aspects of the building's original purpose are still visible, such as the recesses in the exposed stone walls where hens would once have nested.

Located at the end of a long drive, set amidst a developing series of gardens and surrounded by bands of mature trees, this farmhouse is today a magical discovery in one of the loveliest parts of Ireland. "One of the reasons I bought it," the owner explains, "is because this was a place with soul." That soul had suffered neglect for quite some time but he has now brought it radiantly back to life.

OPPOSITE AND ABOVE: Like the parlor below, the principal bedroom displays a more sophisticated approach to decoration through the use of ornamental plasterwork than was usually found in Irish farmhouses. This suggests its first owners must have been familiar with local residences owned by the gentry and aristocracy.

LEFT: A view from the main bedroom into the upper landing, an exceptionally large space where perhaps children would have been expected to sleep since it was directly above the ground-floor kitchen fireplace and therefore would have been very well heated.

HOMES FOR GENTRY

As novels by the likes of Somerville and Ross or Molly Keane have shown, the Irish gentry was always a rather ill-defined caste, not least because it spanned such a broad spectrum of society. So too did the houses occupied by members of the gentry, ranging from relatively humble properties to the most splendid castles. But most often the gentry lived in houses that were somewhere in the middle of this spectrum, a great many of which were constructed during the course of the eighteenth and nineteenth centuries. As a rule, these are decent, solid buildings with few pretensions to grandeur, but offering a considerable degree of comfort and some touches of idiosyncrasy in their design.

THIS PAGE: What had once been the house's living room now acts as a study for Campbell Bruce and his wife Jacqueline Stanley. Its walls also provide hanging space for at least some of the couple's 400-plus collection of contemporary art, including pictures by John Bellany and Michael Kane seen on the left and right of the fireplace.

THE PEMBROKE ESTATE

DUBLIN

What would eventually grow into the largest and most valuable estate in Dublin began to be amassed by the Fitzwilliam family in the mid-fourteenth century. By the Georgian era, their holdings stretched for many miles from the city center south along the coast and west as far as the Dublin Mountains. However, successive Viscounts Fitzwilliam were slow to undertake development of their property until after 1745 when James FitzGerald, twentieth Earl of Kildare (subsequently first Duke of Leinster) built his townhouse on the edge of their land; as James Fitzwilliam wrote in 1752 to his brother, the sixth Viscount, "What a fine rise your estate will have."

TOP LEFT: Part of the long kitchen to the rear of the house has been turned into a dining area, with the chairs painted cobalt blue and the surrounding walls cheerfully hung with plates, cups, and bric-a-brac.

TOP RIGHT: The first-floor bedroom to the front of the house has been turned into a studio by Campbell. Some years ago, Jacqueline, who also used to paint in the house, built herself a self-contained studio at the end of the back garden.

And indeed such was the case, since during the following years the Fitzwilliams developed the highly admired Merrion and Fitzwilliam Squares together with their network of adjacent streets. Following the death of the childless seventh Viscount, his Irish property passed to a relative in England, George Herbert, Earl of Pembroke. His descendants continue to own what for almost two centuries has been known in Dublin as the Pembroke Estate, albeit today it survives on a much-smaller and less profitable scale than was once the case.

Throughout the nineteenth century, the Earls of Pembroke and their agents encouraged the southward development of the city, as is evidenced by the frequent appearance of place names associated with their family

such as Herbert, Pembroke, and Wilton. The Pembrokes were justifiably considered improving landlords because they insisted on the highest standards in any building work undertaken on their land, even if this meant a reduced revenue return in the short term. They also reinvested much of the money in the provision of facilities such as good-quality roads and footpaths, the provision of clean water, and so forth. And they were always keen to beautify their estate. In 1903 the then Earl of Pembroke provided 32 acres for the provision of a public park, used for an international trade exhibition four years later and ever since known as Herbert Park.

Ground rents on the Pembroke Estate were often higher than elsewhere in the city, and leases frequently shorter, initially only for 99 years although this was later extended to 150 years.

Neither Campbell nor Jacqueline is afraid of using bold colors.

Strict conditions were attached to such agreements, notably that houses built on Pembroke land must conform to certain minimum standards and had to be constructed with materials such as granite and red brick. In addition, all lessees were required to secure the estate's permission before any further development of or alteration to the property. These provisos have ensured south Dublin's nineteenth-century terraces and streets present an inimitably elegant uniformity.

Artists Campbell Bruce and Jacqueline Stanley live in the middle of one such terrace in

OPPOSITE: Neither Campbell nor Jacqueline is afraid of using strong colors inside their home; in fact, she argues that bright shades act as a better backdrop for many of the paintings they own. In the kitchen, a wall has been painted acid green while the hall is a dazzling pink. Above a table in the latter hangs an oil seascape by Irish artist Mick O'Dea.

RIGHT: The walls above the chimneypiece in the sitting room carry a variety of small bronzes by the likes of Linda Brunker and Michael O'Sullivan, while the large canvas to the right, entitled Birds, is by Jacqueline.

Sandymount, a residential district on the coast immediately south of the city center. Both Londoners, they moved to Ireland in 1975 when Campbell was appointed Professor of Fine Art at the National College of Art and Design. Two years later they bought their present home which, together with its immediate neighbors, was built in 1867; in typical Dublin fashion, although the exteriors are identical, each house has a different interior layout and the rear gardens vary greatly in

size. For the first six years, the couple had to pay an annual ground rent of £6 to the Pembroke Estate but in 1983 they were able to buy out the lease. Living next door to them when they first arrived was Alun Owen, the Welsh-born writer best remembered for his screenplay of the 1964 Beatles' film, A Hard Day's Night.

Since both of them work at home, for a long time the house contained two studios: hers on the ground floor and his on the first. However in 1994

OPPOSITE: Further evidence of the couple's eclectic collecting habits is found in their bedroom. To the left of the bed, for example, hangs a framed piece of antique Middle Eastern silk embroidered with gold thread and silver sequins.

FAR LEFT: Campbell and Jacqueline found their Victorian brass bed in an old farmhouse in Kent, "covered in muck."

LEFT: The top of a mahogany chest of drawers supports a diverse range of items including an old hat box, a glazed ewer and water basin, and a watercolor by contemporary Irish artist Cecily Brennan.

Although each house in the terrace has the same exterior, every interior layout is different from that of its neighbor.

Jacqueline had a small free-standing building erected at the end of the garden designed for her by architect Angela Rolfe; this is where she now paints every day.

Another well-known Irish architect, John Meagher, produced the design for the house's large conservatory; "We asked for his advice," Jacqueline explains, "and he offered his services." Double doors were inserted between this space and what is now the house's drawing room, an area distinguished by the large number of artworks it holds. Campbell and Jacqueline estimate they have some 400 pieces in their collection of Irish and British contemporary art, much of it produced by friends, colleagues, and former students. Typically the drawing room is hung with work by, among others, Patrick Scott, Albert Irvin, Sean Scully, and Elizabeth Magill. On one wall can be seen a mirror portrait of Francis Bacon made by Andrew Logan, while above the chimneypiece are small bronzes by Michael O'Sullivan and Linda Brunker. Other notable names in the collection include John Bellany, Robert Ballagh, Cecily Brennan, Michael Mulcahy, Mark Joyce, and Mick O'Dea. Occasionally an item has been acquired through a swap: Jacqueline gave one of her prints to photographer John Minihan in exchange for his portrait of Francis Bacon.

The front ground-floor room, which serves as a joint study, is equally full of artwork, as well as being distinguished by the dazzling color of its orange walls. "We've always used color in our homes," says Jacqueline. "We like paintings hanging on something bright." The same daring can be seen elsewhere in the house, such as in the hallway, which is painted pink, and the kitchen, where a dividing wall of tongue-and-groove paneling is acid green and the rush-seated chairs are cobalt blue. The latter room is also filled with a diverse assortment of china and crockery, more of which can be seen on display on the upper landing.

Eclecticism holds no fear for Campbell and Jacqueline. In fact, they seem to relish the opportunity to break rules and to show how an unorthodox approach to decorating can produce gratifying results. It's just as well the Pembroke Estate never had any say over the conformity of its properties' interiors, since otherwise this house would probably have failed to secure official sanction and Dublin might have lost one of its most colorful homes.

CASTLE DODARD
COUNTY WATERFORD

Described by Professor Roy Foster as the "epitome of Elizabethan adventurer-colonist in Ireland," the English-born Richard Boyle first came to Dublin in June 1588 at the age of 21 with just over £27 in his pocket, together with a gold bracelet worth £10, and a diamond ring which had been given to him by his late mother and which he wore all his life. By the time he died more than half a century later in September 1643, Boyle had become the Earl of Cork and amassed an Irish estate of more than 42,000 acres, making him one of the richest men of the period. Much of his wealth accrued from the towns he developed and the commercial enterprises he established in the south-east of Ireland. Order across his estates was maintained by 13 castles which were garrisoned by retainers—during his lifetime, Boyle is said to have employed over 4,000 people.

OPPOSITE: When the Stephensons were restoring the castle, they raised its roof by five feet and so managed to create a third storey which now holds the main drawing room. Like so much else in the building, the carved wooden fireplace was salvaged from an older property.

LEFT: A caretaker and his family occupy the old stone cottage that stands immediately beside the castle.

ABOVE: Seen across a lake created by the Stephensons more than thirty years ago, the three turreted towers give Castle Dodard a romantic appeal and have the effect of making it look more French than Irish.

Castle Dodard in County Waterford is one of the smaller properties supposed to have been constructed for Boyle. Its purpose may have been to act as a fort against the sheep-stealers of neighboring County Tipperary or perhaps it was just a hunting lodge, since one of the Earl's principal residences, Lismore Castle (today owned by his descendant the Duke of Devonshire), is only five miles away. It certainly took on a defensive nature during the 1641 Rising when Castle Dodard served as an outpost for an associate of Boyle, Sir John Leek, until it was seized by Roman Catholic forces led by James Fitzgerald; in turn, he was forced to cede the castle to Sir Percy Smith of nearby Ballynatray in 1645.

"I went for a drive with my brother and sister-in-law," remembers Pam Stephenson, "and found this house."

But after this date little is known of the place's history over the next three hundred years.

Whatever function it served, Castle Dodard, which lies at the foot of the Knockmealdown Mountains and is surrounded by dense woodland, has always presented a highly unusual appearance, even before it was restored by the present owner Pam Stephenson and her late husband. Of trefoil design, the original building consisted of three turreted towers which give it a distinctly Gallic character. By the time a program of refurbishment started in 1968, the structure had fallen into near–irrevocable disrepair, with the turret roofing almost gone and the walls about to crumble.

Pam Stephenson first came across the castle while holidaying with her mother who owned a house in the neighboring town of Fermoy. Since her marriage in 1942, she and her husband, Colonel Stephenson, had spent many years overseas living in such diverse countries as Egypt, Germany, Cyprus, and Malaysia before they retired to England. She certainly had no

ABOVE AND OPPOSITE: Other than all being densely furnished, the rooms in Castle Dodard share no unifying style or theme. In this instance, a color scheme of gold and white has been used whereas usually the Stephensons preferred a richer palette. Note how a curtain has been extended to act as chair cover.

OPPOSITE AND BELOW: The wooden covered bed now used by Pam Stephenson was rescued from a dump and refurbished. Along with the rest of the room, it has been decorated with a variety of fabrics she collected during the years spent traveling around the world with her late husband.

RIGHT: Castle Dodard has four guest suites, each one with a distinctive character but all showing Pam Stephenson's flair for improvisation, such as this four-poster day bed constructed from a variety of found materials.

"Sell the tennis court," Pam wrote to her husband in 1968. "I've bought a castle in Ireland."

intention of acquiring a home in Ireland on that trip to see her mother, but "I went for a drive with my brother and sister-in-law and found this house. It was just a ruin; we had to cut down briars and climb over a stile, the whole place was very wet." Pam and her brother then went to visit the owner, "a man in a cottage at the top of the road—we found him sitting outside with a sack of potatoes looking at the mountain. He went for a walk with my brother and when they came back I saw them shaking hands. As we were driving off, my brother said, 'Well, you've got it if you want it'." That evening she wrote to her husband in England and added a P.S.: "Sell the tennis court—I've bought a castle in Ireland."

LEFT: As if drawing attention to Castle Dodard's rather French appearance, this bedroom suite has a distinctly Gallic atmosphere, helped by the painted bed and gilt-framed screen.

BELOW: One of Pam Stephenson's more imaginative decorating ideas has been to use an ornate gilt overmantel mirror as a bedhead.

OPPOSITE: The additions made to the original castle by the Stephensons more than doubled the size of the property but internally it is impossible to tell new from old, not least because almost no surface or wall space throughout has been left exposed.

Castle Dodard has grown in an ad-hoc fashion. "We extended the building to include groups of apartments linked by interconnecting stairs in the fashion of an Irish seventeenth-century tower house," says Pam.

At the time of her purchase, she did not plan to spend much time at Castle Dodard, not least because of its uninhabitable condition. The Stephensons began by re-roofing the three original towers but not before they had raised the level of the building by about five feet, thereby creating an additional space; previously the castle had held just two rooms, but now it acquired a third which today serves as the main living room with wonderful views over the surrounding countryside. Initially the couple lived in a caravan in the grounds: "There wasn't even running water—we had to fill containers in Lismore and bring them back here."

Scarcely had work been completed on the main structure than the Stephensons started to make additions to it. "We extended the building to include groups of apartments linked by interconnecting stairs in the fashion of an Irish seventeenth-century tower house." Castle Dodard grew in an ad-hoc fashion as both need and whim dictated, until it reached the present form which, as Pam Stephenson

"I'm an exhibitionist," Pam explains of the house's crammed interior.
"So anything anyone gives me I put on display; I can't bear to hide it away."

OPPOSITE: Given the quantity of objects filling every room, it is just as well that Stephenson says that she likes dusting, "because then I can stroke everything and it brings back memories".

ABOVE: Nowhere is Pam's decorating flair more in evidence than this bed. The diverse elements of nineteenth-century rococo revival headboard of button-quilted velvet, embroidered cover from Pakistan, and baldaquin hung with floral cotton ought to be in conflict, but somehow they manage to harmonize.

remarks, "looks like a child's drawing of a castle." Now it contains four suites, each with a sitting-, bed-, and bathroom.

Outside the same extemporized policy was followed. A lake behind the castle, for example, "just happened. We had to drain a bit around the entrance to the house and that made us rather feel like God so then we created the lake with a bulldozer." Similarly, what began as a small storeroom and garage adjacent to the castle evolved over time into a self-contained house: "I remember saying that if we were going to put on a new roof, why not raise the whole thing and put in another floor?"

It's easy to become lost inside the main building as different stairs lead to different sections without access being available between them; visitors to the place need to be fit as there is a lot of ascending and descending involved. But the effort pays off since the interior has been decorated in a singularly eclectic style. Castle Dodard is a repository of global reminiscences, filled with souvenirs of the Stephensons' many years traveling around the world. "I'm an exhibitionist," Pam explains, "so anything anyone gives me I put on display; I can't bear to hide it away." Fortunately, "I quite like dusting because then I can stroke everything and it brings back memories." Castle Dodard today is a storehouse of memory, some of it visible but just as much, going all the way back to the time of Richard Boyle, Earl of Cork, is still waiting to be uncovered.

HIGGINSBROOK
COUNTY MEATH

Rising amid the sleepy, flat pastureland of County Meath, Higginsbrook has been occupied by successive generations of the same family since 1725 when Ralph Higgins settled here and over a period of 18 years used the stones of a ruined tower house to build himself a new home: inserted into the western gable is a stone inscribed, "This house built by Ralph Higgins in ye year 1743." A sundial in the garden is of precisely the same date.

OPPOSITE AND ABOVE: The drawing room retains many original features, such as the timbered paneling to dado rail height and the egg-and-dart decoration on the deep cornice; other than as a decorative detail, there appears to be no purpose to the arched recess on one wall. The rough-finished walls and unadorned door frames reveal the building's early date, before elaborate ornamentation came to be popular in Irish houses.

ABOVE RIGHT: As is attested by an inscribed stone, Higginsbrook was completed in 1743 and must have looked highly sophisticated at the time. Unfortunately no architect is known to have been responsible for the design.

The present occupants comment on the building's curious location so close to the river Boyne, which meant that both the surrounding land and even on occasion the house itself were subject to seasonal flooding until drainage works took place in the mid-1970s. Even more oddly, not a single window in Higginsbrook looks onto the river, as though the builder's intention were to ignore this source of future problems.

Instead the house faces across a miniature park toward a screen of trees that conceals another Higgins house of later date, built after Ralph's grandson had quarreled with his father; as a gesture of defiance this second property, Harcourt Lodge,

LEFT: When inherited by the present owners, little of the house's old furniture remained but they have gradually acquired appropriate pieces such as this fine eighteenth-century mahogany bureau bookcase and a number of charming landscape oils that hang on the walls.

BELOW AND OPPOSITE: The house's study/library is a snug space added onto one of Higginsbrook's gable-ends at some later date. It eloquently demonstrates how, despite the building's extremely grand façade, it is actually a rather modest family home.

The poet F. R. Higgins once described his family home as
"A house of ghosts ... among gardens where even the Spring is old."

has its back turned firmly on Higginsbrook. Evidently the Higginses were given to family disputes since in the early part of the twentieth century Frederick Robert Higgins also fell out with his relatives then living in the old house. A participant in the Irish literary revival, F.R. Higgins was a distinguished poet and a friend of many other writers of the period such as W.B. Yeats, Douglas Hyde, and Austin Clarke (just as his ancestor Ralph must have known Jonathan Swift who was rector of the nearby parish of Laracor during the period Higginsbrook was under construction). In 1936, five years before his early death, he was made director and later business manager of Dublin's Abbey Theatre. Although he loved his native county and often wrote of it, the bad blood between Higgins and his relatives meant the only reference to them in his verse comes in a work called "The Auction," where he disparagingly mentions "feather-brainlings." They in turn were little enamored with the clever but sometimes difficult writer, and even took umbrage after his death when the Dublin literary coterie attending his funeral (including Samuel Beckett) unwittingly trampled over the old family gravestones at Laracor.

The family's internecine disputes have thankfully left no trace on Higginsbrook, described by F.R. Higgins as "A house of ghosts...among gardens where even the Spring is old." If there

are ghosts, then they must have benign dispositions because more than 250 years after its completion, the building still greets visitors with the same serene countenance that would have been familiar to its begetter in the 1740s.

Higginsbrook has an impressive five-bay, two-storey façade, the central section advanced and finished with a pediment above a plain semi-circular window. The entrance doorway is equally fine, with a molded limestone surround and pediment; the brass doorknocker is original to the property, while a bell hanging to one side came from a now-ruinous linen factory erected about a mile away by Joseph Thomas Higgins in 1800. But the impression initially conveyed by Higginsbrook is deceptive, since the house is actually of more modest proportions than its frontage might suggest. The Higginses were never particularly wealthy, their income coming from an adjacent mill that used the rushing waters of the Boyne to felt and scour wool produced by local weavers. This industry probably

ABOVE AND OPPOSITE: The creation of a printroom was a popular form of decoration in eighteenth-century Ireland. It also provided a welcome occupation for women on the many days when it would be too wet to venture outdoors. Although only recently created by the house's owners, the Higginsbrook printroom is in keeping with the spirit of the original concept, down to each picture being given its own "frame" and to spaces between being filled with swags and bows. The dining table has been in the house since the 1770s, but the chairs with their woven rush seats were acquired at a later date.

RIGHT: A collection of hats for use by guests of Higginsbrook's highly sociable owners.

continued only until the time of Ireland's Great Famine in the 1840s, since in 1854 a Valuation report of the area refers to there being "two pairs of stones, one for shelling and one for grinding" at Higginsbrook, suggesting the mill was now used for corn grinding.

The most prosperous Higgins was probably another of Ralph's grandsons, the aforementioned Joseph Thomas who had no less than 15 children and who was a local magistrate and coroner, Poor Law Commissioner, will maker, and Oath-of-Supremacy-taker for the neighboring Roman Catholic gentry. How all his offspring fitted into Higginsbrook with any degree of comfort is an inexplicable riddle as the house is only one room deep and none of those rooms could be considered large. In fact, the single greatest space is devoted to a fine staircase with deep treads, lit by

In the late eighteenth century, one Higgins' forebear somehow lived in the house with fifteen children.

OPPOSITE AND LEFT: The first-floor bedrooms contain even less decoration than downstairs, with just a plain cornice and no dado rail. Despite appearances to the contrary, the delightful dolls' house is not old but was made only a few years ago for the film *Becoming Jane* in which Higginsbrook appeared as family home of the nineteenth-century novelist Jane Austen.

ABOVE: Higginsbrook's age is evident on the upper landing where, after more than 250 years, walls and floor have shifted leaving everything intact but slightly out of kilter.

a large Venetian window; perhaps some of the 15 were expected to sleep in truckle beds here? To the immediate left of the entrance hall lies a pretty drawing room with two deep window embrasures complete with their original, now well-weathered, shutters. Ornamentation here, as throughout the house, is simple: nothing more than some deep egg-and-dart molding around the cornice. The room beyond, a later addition to Higginsbrook's fabric, serves as a cozy study/library. Meanwhile to the hall's right runs a short passage leading to the dining room—where the same mahogany table has been in use for meals since the 1770s—and to service areas beyond. The first-floor bedrooms are laid out on a similar ground plan and are equally unadorned. The charm of Higginsbrook lies not in its decoration but in the house's inviting patina of age and to

Despite its impressive pedimented exterior, Higginsbrook is actually a rather modest house, only one room deep and built for a family whose income derived from mills on the adjacent river Boyne.

ABOVE AND OPPOSITE: As an indication of Higginsbrook's diminutive proportions, the greater part of the master bedroom is taken up by an antique brass and iron bed. Somehow the room also manages to hold an overflow of the owners' many books and part of their collection of old china.

LEFT: In their bathroom, the owners have fitted a sink into an antique chest of drawers, its top covered with a sheet of polished marble.

an awareness that the place has served as home to successive generations of the same family. Over the passage of time, many of the wooden floorboards have become a little lopsided, and so too have door- and windowframes.

The present owners have wisely resisted any temptation to engage in a program of modernization and instead chose to acquire pieces of glass, china, and prints contemporaneous with the house's construction. Higginsbrook today remains replete with the inviting scents of peat fires and baking bread, just as it has done over the past two and a half centuries.

OPPOSITE: Looking through the hall to the living room. "I used to take the innards out and hang them over the range in the kitchen to dry out if there was going to be a concert," says Mari Saville of the old upright piano, "but now it's too far gone for that."

RIGHT: The damp climate of the west Ireland coast means vegetation constantly threatens to overwhelm the house.

BELOW: Almost everything in the house came from somewhere else: the living room's oak fireplace from a house in nearby Kylemore and the 1930s sofa covered in printed velvet bought for just a few pounds.

LETTERFRACK
COUNTY GALWAY

The Irish word "Leitir" means rough hillside and "Fraig" in Old Irish is the word for woman. It would appear that from these two derives the name of the picturesque west Ireland village Letterfrack, which lies at the head of Ballinakill harbor and serves as an entry point to the Connemara National Park.

Until the middle of the nineteenth century, this part of the country was exceptionally poor and neglected. But in 1849, almost immediately after the conclusion of the Great Famine, a wealthy English Quaker couple called James and Mary Ellis bought the lease to a 1,000-acre estate in the area and embarked on its improvement. Among their most lasting achievements was the creation of Letterfrack itself; the Ellises employed some 80 local men to drain bogland, plant thousands of trees, and construct roads and walls. Around the site of a long-established crossroads, they supervised the construction of a two-storey school and Quaker meeting house, a dispensary, a temperance hotel, and a shop, as well as stone cottages for their employees. And although James Ellis's poor health meant he and his wife had to return to England after just eight years—departing, as she wrote, with "a feeling of the much we have left undone, and the darkness which exists there, where nature looks so fair"—Letterfrack survives as a lasting testament to their philanthropy.

It also deserves to be celebrated as the place where in 1913 the pioneer of the modern radio, Guglielmo Marconi (who eight years earlier had married a daughter of Edward O'Brien, fourteenth Baron Inchiquin) set up a transatlantic wireless receiver station for his wireless service; at the same time he erected a near-identical receiver station at Louisbourg, Nova Scotia which sent messages across the ocean. More recently, in 1987 a former industrial school for boys run by the Christian Brothers in the village was converted into a furniture college. This has since become renowned for producing some of contemporary Ireland's most notable craftspeople. Today, Letterfrack is best known as a vibrant holiday destination sited in one of the country's most scenic areas.

The wild, unyielding beauty of the Connemara landscape has always exerted a powerful draw and it acted as an irresistible magnet for Mari Saville when she was seeking a home in Ireland. At the time she was living not far away at Renvyle, where her parents had spent their honeymoon and with which she was familiar from childhood onward. Passing in the vicinity of Letterfrack, she regularly noticed a house outside the village; dating from the 1890s, it had been built for the local doctor

TOP LEFT: A warm day allows the front door to be opened and sunshine to fill the entrance hall, spilling light across the old floor tiles.

TOP RIGHT: A plate rack hung in the kitchen allows Mari Saville to display some of her collection of china, or delft as it is often called in Ireland.

OPPOSITE: One of Mari's cats perches on the Stanley oven. Since the main part of the house has no central heating, the kitchen is always the warmest room in the building and the place to which animals and humans both gravitate.

but had not been occupied since the late 1950s. Although reluctant to sell, the owner was eventually persuaded to do so in 1984 when Mari Saville bought the building and some 20 acres of immediate land.

Since that date, she has spent as much time living in the house as is allowed by her London architectural salvage business, Fens Restoration. A lot of the experience and materials required to restore the Letterfrack property have come from her company and both were needed in abundance. "There were cattle grazing in the kitchen," she recalls. "Everything was gone inside except the tiles on the hall floor. Most of the plaster had already fallen off the walls, so I just took down the rest." Holes in the roof meant that it had been leaking badly for years. "It had dried out, but then the timbers shrank and the roof caved in." All 32 windows had to be replaced and new doors installed.

> "Most of the plaster had already fallen off the walls so I just took down the rest," recalls Mari.

Even post-refurbishment, the house can still be intensely cold since it has no heating other than open fires. And Irish damp has the ability to permeate the thickest of walls. Of the upright piano in the living room, Mari says, "I used to take the innards out and hang them over the range in the kitchen to dry out if there was going to be a concert, but now it's too far gone for that." In the late 1990s, she added a small wing onto the building; since this contains central heating, its study and two bedrooms are mostly used during the winter. Comfortable though the wing may be, it lacks the views available in the main house which stands high on a headland with incomparable views of the bay below and far beyond. Though the demands of her business mean she must return regularly to London, Mari tries to spend as much of the year as she can in her Connemara house, not least because it is also home to two cats and a dog, while in a field outside can be seen her two prized cattle, Liberty and Daphne.

Having trained as a sculptor at the Chelsea School of Art, Mari had the idea of creating a studio for herself on the first floor but that has yet to come about.

OPPOSITE AND BELOW: The house's two principal reception rooms are to the front and both have deep bays with long sash windows. These were designed both to maximize the amount of light entering the rooms and to make the most of the views: the building sits on a high promontory looking across the bay and thence out to the Atlantic Ocean.

Instead, the house is used for entertaining and to provide accommodation for its owner and her guests during the warmer months of the year. A distinctive characteristic of its decoration is that everything in the place is old and usually has a memorable past. "It all fits together and has a story," Mari comments. Some items, such as the dining room table and chairs, belonged to her mother. Many of the electrical goods have been carefully preserved by Mari from her childhood. The International Harvester Company fridge, for example, was one of only four imported from the United States into Ireland some 60 years ago and is likely to be the last still in use. Likewise the toaster in the kitchen has been in service for at least half a century—"Everything's older than I am," says Mari. An inveterate recycler, her home is full of items picked up for little or nothing. The oak fireplace in the living room came from a house in nearby Kylemore, while the 1930s sofa covered in its original printed velvet was acquired for just a few pounds. This house proves a generous imagination is more important than a big budget.

PREVIOUS PAGES: While much of the house was furnished with items acquired through Mari Saville's architectural salvage business, she also inherited some pieces such as the furniture in the dining room which, she says, she has kept for sentimental reasons.

ABOVE AND OPPOSITE: When Mari Saville bought her home, rainwater coming through holes in the roof had caused most of the plaster to drop from the walls and ceilings. It has never been replaced, leaving the rough hewn stone, brick surrounds and timber beams exposed. Although everything from her washing machine to her bath could be classified as antique, it is all still in perfect working order.

RIGHT: Guests are permitted a little more explicit comfort than their hardy hostess and in this bedroom the walls have been plastered and the old brass bed covered in plenty of blankets and quilts.

THIS PAGE: In the drawing room, a black Kilkenny marble chimneypiece original to the house features the crest of the Roberts family, also seen above it in a frame to the right of an early nineteenth-century oil of Maria Odell and her son; Lesley Roberts' mother was a member of the Odell family.

MOUNT RIVERS
COUNTY CORK

Now a dormitory town for Cork city, Carrigaline was for centuries a small, single-street village where the main employment came from local corn and flax mills. These were operated by successive generations of the Roberts family, the original member of which, the Rev. Thomas Roberts, had moved from England to Ireland in the 1630s. Until 1927 his successors lived at Kilmony Abbey, near Carrigaline, but in 1784 William Roberts acquired a house called Mount Rivers which had been built some twenty years before by a wealthy Cork merchant, James Morrison. Today Lesley Roberts is the sixth generation of his family to live in Mount Rivers.

BELOW: On a staircase lined with paintings and prints is hung an oil of the Virgin Mary painted around 1820 by Wilhelmina Westropp, who married into the Roberts clan. The profile portrait directly below shows a member of the Shackleton family to which the Roberts family is also related.

RIGHT: A glimpse of Mount Rivers through the trees in the small garden that still surrounds the old house.

The building is of unusual design since its façade originally had a recessed center between two projections with curved corners. In the 1830s the central space was filled in, a portico added, and a third storey given to the house. However the outer ends of Mount Rivers still retain their rounded windows and the ground-floor porch is a convex-sided recess.

Mount Rivers never had much land attached and its owners were always businessmen, some more successful than others. Lesley Roberts is especially attached to the memory of his great-grandfather, Michael Hodder Joseph Roberts, who, despite enduring innumerable setbacks in both his professional and personal life, continued to struggle on: "One quality our family possesses is tenacity," observes his descendant.

After the mills were finally closed, in 1928 Lesley Roberts' grandfather, Hodder, converted some of the old buildings into a pottery, having noted that bricks were already being made not far away. He took a sample of Carrigaline clay to the famous English potteries of Stoke-on-Trent to see whether it were possible to interest any of the established businesses there in his project but met with no support and was about to leave when, through a local landlady, he was

IN
LOVING MEMO[RY]
OF
THE REV[D] BENJAMIN W[...]
FOR 29 YEARS THE RECTO[R]
WHO DIED 5TH APRIL 18[..]
AND OF ABBY HIS WIFE WHO DIED
AND OF THEIR DAUGHTER ANNE WILLIAMS

PREVIOUS PAGE LEFT: The drawing room's simple stucco frieze beneath the cornice was installed by Lesley Roberts and was copied from that in the morning room at Hoddersfield, a now-lost family house. Likewise the writing desk in the center of the room came from another demolished house, Horsehead, in nearby Passage West. The Gothic-style mahogany bureau bookcase is one of a pair made in Cork in the early nineteenth century and has been in Mount Rivers ever since.

PREVIOUS PAGE RIGHT: Every available surface bears evidence of Lesley Roberts' collecting passion, as can be seen by the heaped top of a mahogany William IV sofa table. Next to it is a cabinet used for storing as many of Lesley's postmarked envelopes as will fit within its drawers and cupboards, although some have spilled out onto the floor.

TOP LEFT: Part of Lesley Roberts' own collection of Carrigaline pottery, the successful business begun by his grandfather in 1928.

TOP RIGHT: A variety of items of significance to Lesley, such as the small oval photograph of his father and uncle that originally belonged to their mother, and shells picked up on the island of Inishboffin.

OPPOSITE: Mount Rivers' entrance hall features a carved mahogany table dating from 1712 that came from the church of Mourne Abbey; the chairs to either side have always been in the house. On the floor rests a funerary monument, one of several in the building that Lesley Roberts rescued from churches that have been demolished or unroofed. Beside it sits the keystone for Britfieldstown, another vanished Roberts house.

introduced to a young pottery designer called Louis Keeling. The latter took Roberts' clay and used it to make a teapot; today that item stands in the drawing room at Mount Rivers. Initially employing just Louis Keeling and six workers, the Carrigaline Potteries proved to be an outstanding success and grew to have a 250-strong workforce. Demand for its wares meant that by the end of the 1930s it became necessary to import clay from the south of England, with boats traveling up the river Owenabue and docking at Carrigaline. While much of the output was strictly functional, it was also distinguished by the beautiful color of the glazes, in particular a lustrous turquoise that remains highly distinctive.

Although the business continued through various travails into the new millennium, after Hodder Roberts' death in 1952 the family had little involvement in the pottery. As for Mount Rivers, it had been left to Lesley Roberts' older brother but at the age of 21 he gave up his

interest in the family home. "Around the same time, I was showing a lot of interest in the house; finding my great-grandfather's diaries from the 1850s onward really fired my enthusiasm." And so it was agreed that Mount Rivers should pass to Lesley who now says, "Youth is a great thing—it blinds you to the problems ahead." And Mount Rivers had plenty of problems, since it had not been occupied by a member of the Roberts family since the early 1950s. Instead the house was let to tenants; there were 15 of them living on the ground floor alone. When these all moved out in 1974, the building was condemned by the local authority as being unfit for human habitation but this did not deter Lesley Roberts, and nor did the amount of work that lay ahead to turn Mount Rivers back into a family home. One of the tenants, he recalls, had drilled holes in the hall ceiling to release rainwater that had come into the house through gaps in the roof and as a result of the constant damp, the ceiling on the floor above had partially collapsed.

Even before he embarked on his program of restoration, Lesley Roberts already felt what he calls "a tremendous affection" for the place that had belonged to his ancestors for the past two centuries. "It's a precious survivor,"

When Lesley Roberts took over his family home, the building had recently been condemned as unfit for human habitation.

OPPOSITE AND RIGHT: A passionate bibliophile, Lesley Roberts is especially interested in books relating to family history, houses, and architecture, "and places and stamps." All these subjects are well represented on the shelves that line the top-floor landing, which also contains a nineteenth-century prayer desk. On the back wall to the right hangs an engraving of his great-grandfather, Michael Hodder Joseph Roberts with whom he feels a particular affinity, while above the door is an old Irish post office sign.

he explains. "There's only one other house around here that has been in the same family for as long; I love the fact that it's still standing." Since taking on the role of Mount Rivers' savior, he has also started to salvage what he can of other buildings that once belonged to members of his family. The weather slating on the exterior of Mount Rivers, for example, came from a now-demolished house called Hoddersfield. Similarly the limestone step outside the back door came from the front door of another now-lost property, Britfieldstown, which stood at a place directly associated with the family, Roberts Cove. Inside Mount Rivers, filling drawers and cabinets and covering the top of every surface are innumerable items collected by Lesley Roberts, each of them carefully tagged with information on their origins. Many but

Lesley is an inveterate and insatiable collector and the house
is filled with items relating to the Roberts family.

by no means all are connected in some way with his forebears; a piece of
cut stone came from the site of the former home of Cork writer Elizabeth
Bowen: "It was asking to be taken," he remarks.

In truth, Lesley Roberts is an inveterate and insatiable collector and
items linked to his family's history provide only one of several outlets
for his zeal. A room on the top floor of Mount Rivers is filled with boxes
containing tens of thousands of postmarks, mostly Irish. Then there is
his collection of old signatures and "anything to do with Irish country
houses—letters, bookplates, things like that." But overriding all else is his
obvious devotion to the house that he has rescued from ruin and brought
back to life. His wife and younger daughter he describes as tolerant of
this commitment to Mount Rivers, but it has been inherited by his older
daughter who, he says, is equally keen on preserving the family home.
Mount Rivers is secure for another generation.

ABOVE AND OPPOSITE: The master
bedroom is dominated by a half
tester bed bought by Lesley Roberts.
To its right hangs a mid-nineteenth-
century portrait of Lydia Roberts
who married a member of the
Westropp family. Over the stone
chimneypiece is an oil of George,
third and last Baron Mount Sandford
of Castlerea, County Roscommon;
exceptionally he was not related in
any way to the Robertses.

THE DEEPS
COUNTY WEXFORD

Touring Ireland in 1835, the Scottish landowner Robert Graham wrote in his journal of "a beautifully situated cottage on a fine reach of the Slaney belonging to Mr Redmond, banker of Wexford." Then known as Newtown Lodge but today called The Deeps, that so-called cottage still stands in the same beautifully situated spot. The external appearance of this Regency villa suggests it ought to be located further east than just a few miles from the Irish Sea.

The long, low façade of the house evokes one of the more remote regions of the former British Empire, the line of shuttered French windows looks ready to be flung open for cocktails on the terrace served by turbaned servants prior to a dinner of curry and gossip about the colonel's wife. But The Deeps was constructed for a branch of one of the County Wexford's best-known local families, the aforementioned Redmonds, one member of which, John Redmond, rose to national prominence at the start of the twentieth century as leader of the Irish Parliamentary Party. By then the family had

LEFT: Tucked around to one side of the main façade, the entrance door is surprisingly modest. It still retains its original brass knocker.

ABOVE: Approached by means of a long drive, The Deeps presents a long, low façade of columns and pilasters. It was probably altered during the nineteenth century, as indicated by the fact that there are two window bays to the right of the veranda portico, but only one to the left.

OPPOSITE: Running across much of the front of the house, the drawing room was originally two rooms but at some date these were made into a single space, today large enough to contain some of the Pearsons' collection of furniture.

OPPOSITE: The entrance hall leads into a long central corridor with a sprung vaulted ceiling lit by three glass domes.

THIS PAGE: Another view of the drawing room. The eighteenth-century chimneypiece was evidently moved from another house to the The Deeps at the time of the latter's construction.

ABOVE LEFT AND CENTER: As a young man, Peter Pearson was not especially interested in Georgian architecture. However, he has said that in the 1970s, "I got upset seeing piles of cut granite from demolished buildings being thrown into Dun Laoghaire harbor." He began to rescue items from properties being taken down and was a pioneer of Ireland's architectural movement. The corridor here is lined with some of his collection of plaster decorative items that came from eighteenth-century buildings that no longer exist.

long since left The Deeps which passed through a variety of hands—and uses—before being bought by Peter and Phil Pearson. When they assumed ownership, the house desperately needed a complete overhaul; over the past few years The Deeps has been re-roofed, rewired, and re-plumbed. Large tracts of the surrounding gardens have been cleared, a couple of tatty lean-tos removed, and a thriving colony of hens and geese established. In addition to these fowl, the Pearsons keep cattle, pigs, and goats on their 45 acres of land, they have an orchard of apple and pear trees, and grow a variety of soft fruits plus a wealth of vegetables.

Much of this activity takes place inside the walled garden which has highly unusual curves at each of its corners. A lot has been achieved,

but just as much remains to be done. A fine yew walk has still to benefit from some attention, the pedimented stable block requires further work, and some of the main house's external cornicing will have to be replaced sooner rather than later.

Although the house might be called The Deeps, the Pearsons' pockets are better described as shallow. A highly esteemed conservationist, author, and painter, Peter explains, "Unfortunately when we came here initially we weren't in a position to do anything at all. It was just after 9/11 and we still hadn't sold our house in Dublin. So we just had to move in, live with the problems, and gradually work around them." This was no easy task. To take one instance, the kitchen—darker than ought to have been the case due

ABOVE RIGHT: The corridor that runs down the center of the house is its most distinctive architectural feature. Doors open to the right onto the study, the drawing room, and, at the top, the morning room, while those on the left provide access to the principal bedrooms.

THIS PAGE AND OPPOSITE: Like the adjacent drawing room, the morning room contains an eighteenth-century chimneypiece that must have come from another, earlier house. Its classical motifs tie in with the moldings on the door panels. On the walls, topographical prints and landscape paintings alternate with more pieces from the Pearsons' collection of architectural salvage.

to later extensions immediately beyond its windows—suffered from such chronic damp the entire floor had to be taken up and a proper damp course laid.

When it came to restoration, one advantage the Pearsons enjoyed over almost anyone else embarking on a similar project was that they could draw on Peter's remarkable collection of architectural salvage, historic items that he has accumulated over decades for no reason other than personal interest. Much of the glass in the house's newly-reinstated sash windows, for example, came from Dublin Castle when part of that complex was undergoing refurbishment. Likewise, inside what was probably once the house's morning room, the main window's frame and shutters both look original but are, in fact, made from old pieces retrieved from various sources by Peter. Downstairs next to the kitchen (now warm and snug and with no hint of its former miserable state), he and Phil have created a charming paneled dining room almost entirely from salvaged material; its pretty Gothic window looking into the hall passage came from a house in County Dublin, while the Gothic cupboard door was rescued from a disused paper mill.

The stylistic features of this room find an echo in the house's façade because while from a distance The Deeps proposes the unadulterated appearance of a classical villa, closer inspection reveals one of its quirks: on either side of the main colonnaded façade are

OPPOSITE: On the lower floor, the Pearsons have created a dining room out of what had been a dark and damp pantry, using a mixture of old and new paneling on the walls; it is now impossible to tell which is which. The window onto the passage beyond came from a house on the outskirts of Dublin.

TOP LEFT AND TOP RIGHT: No piece of salvage is considered too small or insignificant to be of interest to Peter Pearson, who is the author of several books chronicling the architectural history of Dublin and its southern suburbs.

RIGHT: Filled with pieces of old glass and silver, this neo-Gothic cupboard was rescued from the former paper mills at Saggart, County Dublin which closed in 1968 after 200 years of business.

windows with Gothic tracery. Furthermore, the side closest to the principal door has only one bay but there are two at the other end of the front. Idiosyncrasies of this kind indicate The Deeps was extended and altered on several occasions.

The earliest evidence for the Redmond family's association with the place is 1777 and at least part of the present structure probably dates from around that time. The house was then greatly extended in the early nineteenth century, one of the most attractive extant elements from that period being the pair of shallow bow windows to the rear. Further work took place around 1880 with the addition of servants' quarters.

Another notable aspect of the house is its deceptive size. From the exterior, The Deeps looks like a relatively modest summer pavilion whereas it is a substantial house. In a corridor outside the kitchen a line of bells to summon servants indicates that in the nineteenth century there was a drawing room, dining room, smoking room, morning room, and at least six bedrooms—but only one bathroom. Along the center of the house runs a wide pilastered corridor with sprung vaulting that finishes in three oval top lights. Some of the rooms that open off it retain more original features than others; the two main reception areas—

OPPOSITE: In addition to his many other talents, Peter Pearson is a much-admired artist specializing in landscapes and urban prospects as well as murals.

ABOVE: A view of the corridor on the lower floor which would originally have been the preserve of servants but which the Pearsons have made into the center of family life.

LEFT: Peter and Phil Pearson's bedroom on the upper floor. Like all the other bedrooms, this is to the rear of the house and is lit by a wide, shallow bay window looking toward the walled garden.

> When it came to restoration, the Pearsons were able to draw on their collection of architectural salvage.

one of them created when two smaller spaces were knocked together—contain superb eighteenth-century Adamesque chimneypieces that look as though they were brought from a larger house. Sadly most of the old floors are gone, replaced forty-odd years ago by harsh parquet; the boards that did survive were buried beneath linoleum. Similarly a lot of the house's shutters and window entablatures were also pulled out by previous owners. Thanks to the labors of a first-class local joiner, these are gradually being replaced.

The worst of onerous restoration now behind them, the Pearsons can start to turn their attention to more pleasant tasks, such as choosing colors for walls—when, that is, they are able to take a break from other duties, such as collecting fuel for the wood-burning stove that can heat their home, hacking back invasive bamboo, protecting soft fruit from the birds, constructing a new woodshed, minding their livestock, and tending the vegetable garden.

THE BIG HOUSE

IN IRELAND, THE BIG HOUSE IS A GENERIC TERM USED TO DESCRIBE THE MOST IMPORTANT RESIDENCE IN AN AREA. THE BIG HOUSE HAS BEEN ADMIRED, ENVIED, AND ABHORRED IN EQUAL MEASURE AND THE IRISH LANDSCAPE IS ROMANTICALLY LITTERED WITH ITS ABANDONED RUINS. BUT WHILE THE TOLL HAS BEEN HEAVY OVER THE PAST HUNDRED YEARS, A SURPRISING NUMBER OF THESE HOUSES REMAIN TO THIS DAY, SOME RESCUED AND RESTORED BY NEW OWNERS, OTHERS STILL IN THE HANDS OF THEIR ORIGINAL FAMILIES. THE MERITS OF THE BIG HOUSE WERE NOT ALWAYS APPRECIATED, BUT THERE IS NOW BETTER UNDERSTANDING OF THESE BUILDINGS' PLACE IN IRISH HISTORY AND ARCHITECTURE. THEIR FUTURE CERTAINLY LOOKS MORE SECURE THAN EVER USED TO BE THE CASE.

LEVINGTON PARK
COUNTY WESTMEATH

Sir Richard Levinge, fourth baronet, was a notable Irish eccentric who, on the occasion of his marriage in 1748, built himself a new home near the town of Mullingar in County Westmeath. Believed to be to Sir Richard's own design, the house, called Levington Park, had a number of unusual features, such as a series of holes in the ceiling joists of his ground-floor bedroom.

These were meant to allow internal access to tendrils from a vine planted immediately outside the south gable-end so that Sir Richard could eat grapes without getting out of bed; unfortunately he seems not to have taken into account the cold damp Irish climate and no grapes ever grew. Meanwhile, his dining room featured a large mirror on its ceiling so that during meals the host could better appreciate the "natural beauties" of his female guests. Again, the venture was doomed to failure since steam rising from dishes on the table tended to fog the glass.

Although somewhat altered by additions made in the early nineteenth and twentieth centuries, Levington Park still stands and since 1972 it has been the home of eminent Irish-American writer J.P. Donleavy; prior to moving here, the author of such works as *The Ginger Man* and *The Beastly Beatitudes of Balthazar B* had been living in the adjacent county of Meath. Levington's previous owner was Donleavy's contemporary at Trinity College, Dublin and with his

OPPOSITE: The morning room is the only one in Levington Park to have retained its original mid-eighteenth century decoration, not least the delightful rococo frieze decorated with flower baskets and swags of foliage, as well as the low chair rail running around the walls.

LEFT: The rear aspect of the house probably looks much as it did when first constructed by Sir Richard Levinge in the 1740s. Wings at 90-degree angles to the main block create a long, narrow courtyard in which a later owner created a small canal, thereby giving the space a focal point.

ABOVE: The morning room's walls are covered in a chinoiserie-style paper such as would have been popular in Ireland at the date of the house's construction. The rococo taste lasted longer in Ireland than in England and it was only toward the closing decades of the eighteenth century that it was superseded by neo-classicism.

Built for and by an eccentric, Levington Park is decidedly idiosyncratic.

American wife he had installed not just an abundance of bathrooms—nine altogether—but also an indoor heated swimming pool. Evidently the presence of these facilities helped to secure the sale, as did the fact that no restoration work had to be done to the building—and nor has any had to be undertaken since. No longer married, Donleavy observes, "I suppose the place has suffered a little as I've never taken much interest in major restoration. A woman would normally react and say this or that has got to be done. But because of its many rooms it isn't a place women particularly take to..."

Which is not to suggest that Levington is devoid of charm—in addition to those provided by nine bathrooms and a swimming pool. The latter is accommodated in one of the long ranges that stretch behind the main block and terminate in a range of outhouses, to create a delightful enclosed courtyard down the center of which runs a miniature canal surrounded by grass. How much of this work dates from Sir Richard Levinge's day and how much from later improvements is impossible to tell. Easier to see are the changes made to the front of the house around 1810 when Levington Park was owned by another Sir Richard, the sixth baronet.

At that time the three center bays were given a shallow eaves pediment containing a wide fanlight window, in addition to a Wyatt window on the first floor and below that a deep Doric porte-cochère. Indoors, the two

ABOVE: The drawing room is distinguished by a sequence of tall sash windows set into deep embrasures to accommodate the unusual shutters which are divided into upper and lower sections, thereby allowing the occupant privacy without excluding all light. The large white marble chimneypiece must date from the period when this room was created; a knock on one section of wall to its left reveals it to be of thin wood, suggesting a door used to be there.

OPPOSITE: As remains the case on the other side of the entrance hall, the drawing room was originally two rooms and only assumed its present form after the house was remodeled in the early nineteenth century. The present owner, J.P. Donleavy, spends a great deal of time here. An artist as well as author, he painted almost all the pictures hanging on the walls.

OPPOSITE: With its steeply-pitched roof, Levington House is not a particularly deep house and immediately behind the principal reception rooms runs a vaulted corridor more tall than wide. It is lit by two full-length windows opening onto the rear courtyard. Both on the walls and the floor beneath are further examples of Donleavy's artwork.

TOP AND BOTTOM LEFT: Set behind an arched screen, a cantilevered stone staircase leads to the upper storey where a series of rooms runs off a slim corridor. The latter is distinguished by its flagstoned floor, especially unusual because the floor downstairs is of wood thereby reversing the normal order.

RIGHT: At either end of the main ground-floor corridor, doors open into the wings which would once have been the domain of servants. Beyond the door at the end of this passageway lies the former coachhouse and then a sequence of outbuildings and stables.

The interior of Levington is full of long, lean corridors.

rooms to the left of the entrance hall were made one and the dining room to the far right was given a bow window affording views of Lough Owel, one of the area's many natural lakes, of which J.P. Donleavy owns about half a mile of shoreline.

Although he has a fine study in the house, the writer tends to spend a good bit of his time in the fine drawing room created in 1810. This has a handsome white marble chimneypiece in which a fire seems to be forever smoldering. One of the characteristics of the room are its window shutters, divided vertically into two sections so that the lower part can be closed to provide privacy while the upper remain open to admit plenty of natural light; one wonders whether these might have been installed to satisfy another of Sir Richard's idiosyncrasies. The only decoration here is a refined neo-classical plasterwork cornice border that contrasts with its more exuberant equivalent in the morning room replete with flower baskets and swags.

OPPOSITE: As built by Sir Richard Levinge, the house had an enfilade of five rooms (including the entrance hall) that ran from one end of Levington Park to the other. Though other decorative elements were subsequently altered, the original heavy doorframes remain in situ.

THIS PAGE: Among the structural changes effected to the house around 1810 was the addition of a bow to the end of the dining room, allowing views of nearby Lough Owel, one of the best known lakes in the Irish midlands. In its first incarnation, this room featured a large mirror on its ceiling so that Sir Richard Levinge could better appreciate the "natural beauties" of his female guests. Unfortunately, he failed to take into account the steam rising from dishes on the table which fogged the glass and made it impossible to see anything.

THIS PAGE: The bedrooms in Levington Park, as in the majority of Irish country houses, have a uniform starkness and air of functionality. Worthy of note in this instance, however, are the coved ceilings that increase the height of the rooms and terminate in a heavy molding.

OPPOSITE: Similarly, the chimney-pieces in the first-floor rooms are notable for their want of ornament. What will strike visitors to the house is the number of bathrooms, far more than is the norm in an Irish country house. This was one of the features that appealed to the American-born owner when he bought the place in 1972.

Despite the unpropitious Irish climate, Sir Richard Levinge attempted to train a grape vine through his bedroom window.

The morning room is the sole space in the house to retain its original mid-eighteenth century character, emphasized by the Georgian-style chinoiserie paper covering the walls both above and below the chair rail. The splendid chimneypiece here also dates from the time of the house's construction.

Levington's principal rooms on both ground and first floor all run along the front of the building, behind which are narrow corridors. That on the ground floor has a vaulted ceiling and is lit by a pair of full-length windows opening onto the courtyard. Curiously, while its floor is of timber, that at bedroom level is stone-flagged, a strange reversal of the usual arrangement and one which must have made this passageway always cold underfoot. Access to the upper storey is gained via a flight of wide stairs of cut limestone accessed through a twin-arched screen. On the return stand an elaborately carved, marble-topped table and mirror—some of the few items of furniture Donleavy acquired from Levington's previous owner and which may always have occupied this spot.

If so, they would have been seen by another author believed to have been in the house at the start of the last century. James Joyce's father John, then a civil servant, spent some time in Mullingar compiling a new electoral register of the area.

Joyce came to visit his parent in 1900 and 1901 and on both occasions seemingly stayed at Levington Park which, under the name of "Mr Fulham's house," features in *Stephen Hero*, the precursor of *A Portrait of the Artist as a Young Man*. "It was an odd irregular house, barely visible from the road, and surrounded by a fair plantation," Joyce noted in *Stephen Hero*. "It was reached by an untended drive and the ground behind it thick with clumps of faded rhododendrons sloped down to the shore of Lough Owel..."

Those lines were written just over a century ago but little has since changed and it is likely James Joyce would still recognize Levington Park today, although he would definitely be disconcerted by the nine bathrooms and swimming pool.

TULLYNALLY
COUNTY WESTMEATH

"We, my mother, Lovell, Fanny, and I came here yesterday," the novelist Maria Edgeworth wrote to a friend on January 21st, 1824, "glad to see Lord Longford surrounded by his friends in old Pakenham Hall hospitable style... The house has been completely new-modeled, chimneys taken down from top to bottom, rooms turned about from lengthways to broadways, thrown into one another, and the result is that there is a comfortable excellent drawing-room, dining-room, and library, and the bed-chambers are admirable."

N ow known as Tullynally, the Pakenham Hall described by Edgeworth had already undergone a number of transformations and would experience several more before reaching the form in which it is seen today but now, as then, the principal reception rooms are comfortable and excellent and the bedrooms continue to be admirable. Indeed, the house was deservedly deemed "an early nineteenth-century Gothic Palace" by John Betjeman when the future Poet Laureate stayed there in September 1939. As

OPPOSITE: Tullynally's stupendous entrance hall may date back to the eighteenth century but was given its present decoration in the early 1820s under the direction of James Shiel. In an arched niche can be seen the Pakenham family crest: an eagle rising out of a mural crown.

ABOVE LEFT AND ABOVE RIGHT: Set in the midst of Westmeath's rich countryside, while Tullynally underwent many transformations, it has remained home to generations of Pakenhams since the 1650s.

RIGHT: The house is so extensive that it is easy for visitors to lose their way along the maze of passages that link one section of Tullynally with another.

ABOVE: In a corner of the entrance hall, a large painted box is constantly stocked with firewood: access to ample fuel is essential in any Irish country house.

RIGHT: The drawing room's geometrical design ceiling is another intervention by James Shiel during his remodeling of the house in the 1820s, but the marble chimneypiece dates from an earlier period and reflects the gradual evolution of Tullynally over several centuries.

architectural historian Mark Bence-Jones has observed, "with its long, picturesque skyline of towers, turrets, battlements, and gateways stretching among the trees of its rolling park, Tullynally covers a greater area than any other country house in Ireland," and looks "not so much like a castle as a small fortified town; a Camelot of the Gothic Revival."

Somewhere buried far beneath its romantic carapace of castellations and battlements lies the plain two-storied Georgian house that once served as home to the Pakenham family. Originally from Suffolk, the first of their number to settle in Ireland was Captain Henry Pakenham, who in 1655 accepted a grant of lands in Westmeath, as well as in Wexford, in lieu of arrears of pay. His successors remained

LEFT: Over the chimneypiece in the library hangs a large oil portrait of Major General Sir Edward Pakenham, killed at the age of 36 at the Battle of New Orleans in 1815. During his lifetime he had been known for his bad temper and when his body returned to Ireland in a cask of rum, one relative remarked, "The General has returned home in better spirits than he left."

in the former county and lived in the aforementioned two-storied property which appears in a drawing made in 1738 by George Pakenham. At the time it lay at the center of elaborate formal gardens with canals, basins, and cascades. These would all be swept away in favor of a more "natural" park, although Tullynally's present owners, Thomas and Valerie Pakenham, have created marvelous new gardens filled with plants brought back from trips to China and Tibet.

Thomas believes that the first alterations to his family home were made soon after the

Tullynally is a bibliophile's dream, with every room overflowing with books.

1738 drawing, since a year later his namesake Thomas Pakenham married the heiress Elizabeth Cuffe and it is likely that with her money a third storey was added to the house. That earlier Thomas was created Baron Longford in 1756 and almost twenty years later his widow became Countess of Longford in her own right. While the second Baron Longford's accounts record improvements carried out to the building around 1780 by a Mr Myers, these consisted mostly of raising ceiling heights on the ground floor and changing windows, and it was his son, the second Earl of Longford, who initiated the work responsible for transforming Tullynally from a house into a castle. Though two of his brothers were professional soldiers—Major

Originally a classical house, successive architects transformed Tullynally into a Gothic castle.

General Sir Edward Pakenham whose portrait hangs in the library was killed at the Battle of New Orleans in 1815—and his sister Kitty was married to the first Duke of Wellington, the earl seems to have preferred spending his time carrying out improvements on his Irish property. Between 1801 and 1806 the pre-eminent Irish architect of the period, Francis Johnston, worked

at Tullynally, adding what one observer has since called "little more than a Gothic face-lift for the earlier house," notably two round towers projecting from the corners of the main block and battlements around the parapet. In 1817 the Earl married and no doubt it was the incentive of a new bride and growing family that encouraged him a few years later to embark on a second round of work at Tullynally, this time using Johnston's former clerk, James Shiel. His interventions included the addition of a three-sided bow on

LEFT: Lined with oak shelves, Tullynally's library contains some 6,000 volumes representing 2,000 titles spanning almost four centuries. All of them have been cataloged by Thomas Pakenham.

ABOVE: Evidence of Tullynally's size can be seen in the quantity of keys hanging from hooks in this bureau.

OPPOSITE: The dining room, like most of the other ground-floor rooms in the house, keeps its early nineteenth-century Gothic decoration with wainscoted walls beneath a Perpendicular-style plaster ceiling. Family portraits hang against a Puginesque paper.

the garden front and the Gothicization of the immense hall and adjacent rooms. It was of Shiel's work that Maria Edgeworth wrote in her letter of 1824; long before that date her inventor father (and the Longfords' neighbor) Richard Lovell Edgeworth had devised a revolutionary form of domestic central heating for the building, the first such in Ireland; in 1807, Maria wrote, "the immense Hall is so well warmed that the children play in it from morn till night."

From 1839 to 1842 the third Earl, a bachelor, employed architect Sir Richard Morrison to further embellish Tullynally and to design two castellated wings linking the house with its stable courtyard; a final flourish was added by the fourth Earl in 1860 with the construction of a pinnacled tower at the northern end of the site.

While earlier generations of Pakenhams might have been renowned for their military prowess, over the past century the pen has vanquished the sword. Edward, sixth Earl of Longford, who succeeded to the title while still in his teens, wrote many plays as well as several volumes of poetry. He and his wife Christine were supporters of Dublin's Gate Theatre from 1930 onward and founded the Longford Players. Following his death, he was succeeded by his brother Frank, the well-known British politician and human rights campaigner as well as author. His wife Elizabeth was an historian, as are two of their children, Antonia Fraser and Thomas Pakenham, the present occupant of Tullynally. In turn, his wife Valerie has written several books and their daughter

OPPOSITE AND ABOVE: There seem to be as many bedrooms in Tullynally as there are corridors, all of them the same high-ceilinged spaces with minimal architectural decoration. But the presence of a comfortable chaise longue, a well-sprung bed, and an abundance of good reading material ensure that guests invited to stay in the house rarely wish to leave their allotted rooms.

Despite its vast size, Tullynally manages to
be comfortable and even cozy.

Eliza recently published a history of the family in the late
eighteenth/early nineteenth century.

No wonder, therefore, that a feature of Tullynally is the sheer
quantity of books it contains, not least in the early nineteenth-
century library. Here the walls are lined with oak shelving on
which rest some 6,000 volumes, representing 2,000 titles
spanning almost four centuries. All have been meticulously
cataloged by Thomas, permitting him to trace any work across
14 different fields including author, name, subject, language,
and date of publication. But Tullynally's books are by no means
confined to the library and can be found in profusion throughout
the house. In 1971, as part of his 12-volume roman-fleuve *A
Dance to the Music of Time*, Anthony Powell, who was married
to Thomas Pakenham's aunt Violet (herself another writer),
published the novel *Books Do Furnish a Room*. In the case of
Tullynally, they furnish an entire house, helping to make it one
of the most inviting houses in Ireland.

ABOVE: Creature comforts have often been
rather scarce in the Irish country house and
while food, drink, and conversation are
abundant, visitors should prepare themselves
for a shortage of certain other facilities.
Only since the present owners assumed
responsibility for Tullynally has it acquired
sufficient bathrooms, previous generations
having to make do with just a couple shared
between all the occupants of this very
substantial property.

OPPOSITE: Strong color is a feature of
Irish house interior decoration, perhaps a
reaction to the predominance of gray light
found outdoors for much of the year. This
bold red is typical of the shades found in
many homes throughout the country.

STRADBALLY HALL
COUNTY LAOIS

Ancient Ireland contained five provinces and it was only after the Norman invasion of the late twelfth century that the island started to be divided into smaller counties, the latter eventually numbering 32. Much of this work was undertaken during the sixteenth century when successive Tudor monarchs encouraged English settlers to take over large tracts of land hitherto owned by the unruly Irish. In 1556, for example, Mary I created two new shires in the midlands, named Queen's and King's County after herself and her husband, Philip II of Spain.

OPPOSITE: Though the basic design of the drawing room has remained unaltered since it was constructed in the eighteenth century, a distinctly Victorian atmosphere prevails thanks to the gilt wallpaper put up during that period.

BELOW AND ABOVE LEFT: The exterior of Stradbally was extensively remodeled during the 1860s when architect Charles Lanyon was employed to enlarge the house.

ABOVE CENTER: Among the many quirky features of the house is a large collection of stuffed animals in display cases, including one featuring squirrels engaged in a boxing match.

Queen's County, known as Laois since Ireland gained independence in 1922, exceptionally neither has any sea coast nor borders onto any county which does so; it is therefore considered the most landlocked part of Ireland. However, Laois's rich pastures, woodlands, and mineral resources, as well as its geographical importance, have always given it a special significance. For centuries the area was effectively controled by the O'Moores, the leading family of the region's Seven Septs, the other six being tributary to them. Rory O'More (as it was then spelled) who died in 1557 and his son, Rory Óg O'More, were both notable leaders in Ireland's wars against the Tudors, while another member of the same family, also called Rory O'More, would become head of the 1641 rising against the English. The O'Mores' opponents included successive

generations of Cosbys, beginning with the arrival in Ireland of Sir Francis Cosby, an English soldier who was granted land in Queen's County after being appointed General of the Kern (an armed Irish foot soldier) by Mary I in 1558. Since this land traditionally belonged to the O'Moores, it is not surprising Sir Francis remained in perpetual conflict with Rory Óg until the latter was slain in a battle against English forces in 1577; Sir Francis would himself be killed three years later in the Battle of Glenmalure, where the Irish were led by the celebrated warrior Fiach MacHugh O'Byrne.

Sir Francis was succeeded by his eldest son Alexander, whose home became a former Franciscan friary in Stradbally, Queen's County. The name Stradbally derives from the Irish term An Sráidbhaile, meaning a village or town of one street. And so it remains to this day; Stradbally is effectively a long linear street with two openings on the western side forming Market Square and Courthouse Square. The remnants of the old friary survive, but in the closing years of the seventeenth century the Cosbys built themselves an

ABOVE AND OPPOSITE: The salon is the middle of three interconnecting reception rooms on the garden front of Stradbally. All retain the decoration they were given in the 1770s, an era when the taste for Adamesque neo-classicism became prevalent throughout the country and replaced the more exuberant rococo style that had hitherto been popular. The salon's chaste white marble chimneypiece and restrained cornice frieze bear

witness to the period's taste, even if much of the furniture in the room dates from the nineteenth century. Lining the walls are cabinets and bureaux filled with china and other ornaments accumulated over successive generations.

RIGHT: A giltwood chaise has been placed in a corner of the drawing room beside one of the windows hung with curtains that are now more than a century old.

The eye is led from one stupendous room to the next, each crammed with still more family memorabilia.

OPPOSITE AND ABOVE: The ground-floor suite of reception rooms are linked by centrally-placed arched doorways filled with heavy mahogany doors. At one end lies the dining room, terminating in a massive carved oak sideboard on which stands a line of salvers. While some of the more valuable family portraits have had to be sold, copies still hang on the walls so that the present generation of occupants continues to be observed by their forbears, no doubt amazed that after four and a half centuries there are still Cosbys in residence at Stradbally.

alternative residence, which was then added to and embellished by successive generations before it, in turn, was deemed no longer suitable (the house's appearance is known from an extant topographical painting of Stradbally dating from circa 1740). In 1772 Dudley Cosby, who for his services as British Minister to the Court of Denmark had been created Lord Sydney of Leix and Baron Stradbally, embarked on the construction of a new house on a site about half a mile southwest of the old one, which by then had already been demolished. Within two years Lord Sydney was dead and the incomplete property passed to a cousin, Admiral Philips Cosby, who had been born in America where his father was Lt Governor of Annapolis and his uncle, General William Cosby, Governor of New York. Though Admiral Cosby retired from the Royal Navy in 1782, he was repeatedly recalled to serve during wars against the French.

The house begun by Lord Sydney and completed by his heir forms the core of the present Stradbally Hall; of two storeys over a raised basement and nine bays long, its chaste late eighteenth-century classical decoration survives in the three linked reception rooms on the garden front. But the

building's external appearance was radically altered during the 1860s when Colonel Robert Cosby employed the architect Sir Charles Lanyon to enlarge and remodel Stradbally Hall. A new entrance front was added to the property featuring two-bay projections on either side of a single-storey Doric portico. Meanwhile, on the garden front, the house's existing recessed center section was filled with a stupendous three-arch loggia and a two-storey "bachelors' wing" added to the immediate west. Lanyon also made many changes to the building's interior, not least the creation of a vast, top-lit central hall. This features a Victorian oak staircase climbing up to a picture gallery some sixty feet long and twenty feet wide, above which is suspended

ABOVE AND OPPOSITE: The most distinctive feature of Stradbally's alterations in the 1860s was the creation of an inner hall—the original hall of the eighteenth-century house—leading to a gallery measuring sixty feet by twenty. A staircase of carved and turned oak leads to the first floor, at either end of which are screens of pink marble Corinthian columns below the coffered and elaborately ornamented ceiling. Brass lanterns provide light in the evening and cast a soft glow over family pictures and pieces of old china.

LEFT AND OPPOSITE: Like much of the rest of the house, Stradbally's bedrooms have scarcely changed since the mid-nineteenth century and their furnishings all date from this period. At the time, the Cosbys were extremely wealthy landlords with large estates but even by the 1880s the value of their rental income had begun to fall. Like many landowners, they were eventually obliged to give up much of the estate and with it went the funds which might have been spent on modernizing Stradbally.

a coffered and barrel-vaulted ceiling with glass occupying a considerable part of the space; at either end of the gallery small lobbies were created by the insertion of a pair of pink marble Corinthian columns and each side of the gallery is flanked by a line of bedrooms. Nothing else can match the scale and grandeur of the hall, but some of the ground-floor rooms come close, not least the ballroom which also serves as a library. The most notable feature here is the ceiling, decorated with a series of 24 early nineteenth-century French paper panels telling the story of Cupid and Psyche. While the basic form of the three interconnecting

ABOVE AND RIGHT: All the principal bedrooms have the same large white marble and cast-iron fireplaces which would once have been kept well-stoked by servants. The latter would also have taken care to fill the jugs and basins with hot water since bathrooms were a rarity in nineteenth-century country houses. Many of Stradbally's bedrooms contain watercolor landscapes painted by earlier members of the family.

Few Irish houses are more imbued with the spirit of the nineteenth century.

reception rooms on the garden side remains much as they were when first built in the late eighteenth century, their decoration is now distinctly Victorian, not least thanks to the gilt wallpaper in the drawing room.

Stradbally Hall's size makes it plain that this was a house designed for entertaining on a massive scale. The early nineteenth-century Irish memoirist Sir Jonah Barrington, who was born not far away at Abbeyleix, writes of a dinner at Stradbally Hall during which a half-blind guest sitting next to Admiral Philips Cosby mistook the latter's knobbly fist for a bread roll and thrust his fork into it with easily imagined consequences. Still home to the Cosby family, Stradbally remains an attractive destination, albeit in somewhat different circumstances than during the admiral's time; the estate is now the venue for an annual music festival, the Electric Picnic, which takes place at the end of summer.

ABOVE AND LEFT: The ballroom, which also doubles as library, was the largest single addition made to Stradbally during the house's remodeling in the 1860s. Around its flaking red walls mahogany bookcases are filled with leather-bound volumes, while the ceiling high above is decorated with a series of 24 early nineteenth-century French paper panels telling the story of Cupid and Psyche.

OPPOSITE: Faded chintz and wallpaper typify the bedrooms of Stradbally where the floors are covered in old rugs and the windows hung with curtains of an equal age. Only the light fittings indicate this is not the nineteenth century.

OPPOSITE: After almost two hundred years of warfare and civil strife, the early eighteenth century was a period of calm and confidence in Ireland. Nothing better exemplifies the era's sense of assurance than the palatial houses built in the country's rapidly expanding capital from 1700 onward, of which this is an example.

HENRIETTA STREET

DUBLIN

Although relatively unknown today other than by architectural aficionados, Henrietta Street was once Dublin's grandest thoroughfare and is still lined with houses of princely proportions. Lying north of the river Liffey in a part of the city that has suffered much dereliction, the street was originally laid out in 1729–30 by eighteenth-century Ireland's most imaginative developer, Luke Gardiner, whose descendants would subsequently become Earls of Blessington. Gardiner's ambitions are reflected in the size of the Henrietta Street houses, some of which are four- or five-bay wide, making them considerably larger than other Dublin properties of the time.

ABOVE LEFT AND BELOW: Successive generations, some extremely rich, others miserably poor, have occupied this same house since it was constructed circa 1730. All of them have left their mark on the building, as can be seen by the different patinas of paintwork on the walls of a first-floor room.

ABOVE RIGHT: A bicycle in the hall. At the time it was laid out, Henrietta Street stood at the very edge of Dublin but today is considered as lying within the city center. And given the Irish capital's traffic problems, no doubt this represents the fastest and most convenient way to get about.

As befitted such splendid residences, during the Georgian period Henrietta Street was occupied by some of the wealthiest aristocratic families in the country. Early occupants included the Earl of Bessborough, Viscount Mountjoy, and Lord Farnham; a 1792 city directory lists one archbishop, two bishops, four peers, and four MPs as living in Henrietta Street. But with the decline of Ireland's economic fortunes in the nineteenth century came a corresponding degeneration of this once-prized address. Fallen from fashion, its houses were gradually abandoned by their original owners and acquired instead by landlords who turned the majority of the buildings into tenements. Entire families came to live in partitioned sections of rooms that had once been used for entertaining members of the Irish nobility. Henrietta Street developed

This princely house once served as a tenement slum.

a reputation for being among the worst of Dublin's slum accommodation; some unscrupulous owners even pulled out a number of houses' fine main staircases so that they could squeeze more tenants into their properties. One supporter of the Irish Georgian Society, Ireland's leading voluntary conservation body, remembers visiting the street in the mid-1960s and meeting an old woman who pointed to a house that had been home of sorts to between 200 and 300 people, all of them living in squalor. Another day, he witnessed a pig stagger out of a house, "so badly kept that it could hardly walk. Every few paces its hind legs gave way and it collapsed into a sitting position." In March 1982, the *Irish Times* even reported that until not long before, a horse had lived on the second floor of No. 14 Henrietta Street.

It was only in the last quarter of the twentieth century that this tragic scenario started to change as Dublin's architectural history came to be better understood and awareness grew of Henrietta Street's importance within that context. Houses hitherto allowed to fall into decrepitude were rescued and restored, often by individuals whose enthusiasm exceeded their income. Such is the case with the house featured here, which was bought by its present owner some 25 years ago and has been gradually refurbished as time and funds allowed. The building, together with its neighbor, is among the earliest extant terraced houses in Dublin and dates from 1730–33, when both were erected by Luke Gardiner with the intention of being either rented or sold. A surviving drawing for a stone-cut doorway by

LEFT: One of a pair of reception rooms occupying the greater part of the first floor and designed for entertaining on a princely scale. When the house became a tenement, the original chimneypieces were lost; that shown here was installed by the present owner.

OPPOSITE: A view from the rear reception room through to the landing. Considerable structural modifications were made to the building from 1780 onward when Richard Boyle, second Earl of Shannon, decided to join this house to its immediate neighbor and make one enormous residence for himself. It is likely an opening between the two buildings would have been created where the statue of Apollo now stands.

THIS PAGE: While prints hang on most of the house's walls, those of the rear reception room are decorated with an assortment of oil paintings collected by the present owner. That on the left depicts an early nineteenth-century family group, perhaps showing the visit of a newly-married bride to her unwed siblings.

FAR LEFT: Sitting atop a plain chimneypiece is a splendid gilt rococo mirror of the kind that were highly fashionable in the mid-eighteenth century when this house was still newly-constructed.

LEFT: An early nineteenth-century carved mahogany sofa is covered in woven silk damask of such age that it has become entirely shredded in places.

OPPOSITE: When the Earl of Shannon undertook a refurbishment of the house in the 1780s he employed one of the period's most notable stuccodores, Charles Thorp. Subsequently a Lord Mayor of Dublin, Thorp built himself an equally splendid residence not far away on North Great George's Street. His refined, neo-classical taste can be seen in this room's cornice frieze.

Sir Edward Lovett Pearce suggests that this pre-eminent architect had a hand in the design of the houses, although both have been so much altered since their original construction that little indication remains of how they must have looked when newly-built. Some of the greatest structural modifications occurred from 1780 onward when Richard Boyle, second Earl of Shannon, decided to join the pair in order to make one enormous town residence for himself. Various changes were made to the house under consideration, not least the removal of its main staircase and, on the first floor, the creation of new windows very much longer than their predecessors. The rooms at this level are very simply decorated with late eighteenth-century plasterwork cornices designed by Dublin stuccodore, Charles Thorp. What most impresses a contemporary visitor is their height and volume and the purity of light with which they are imbued.

The Earl of Shannon remained in residence until 1807, after which the two buildings were once more divided. From 1821 this house was occupied by

Lord Shannon's drawing rooms have recovered their grace and elegance.

Captain George Bryan of Jenkinstown Park, County Kilkenny, known as the richest commoner in Ireland, although he suffered a dent in his wealth through the long and ultimately unsuccessful legal claim he made to a dormant Irish peerage. Presumably it was during his time in occupation that the present staircase was installed in the rear hall; its antecedent had been located immediately inside the front door as remains the case next door. Until the close of the twentieth century, Captain Bryan was the house's last owner-occupier since it next became offices for a solicitor and a proctor before passing into the possession of the British War Office which, from 1861 onward, used the premises as headquarters of the City of Dublin Artillery Militia. Following this it went into precipitous decline and

then sunk into an open-door tenement building, remaining such until it was rescued by the current owner.

Inevitably he has had to undertake an enormous amount of work to secure the house, which at the time of his acquisition suffered from dry rot, deteriorating timbers, roof valley decay, and many other serious problems. All of these have since been resolved and the property can now look forward to a secure future. Some internal decoration has also been undertaken, not least the removal of internal partitions which had been fitted in order to accommodate more tenants. The original chimneypieces had long since been taken out and sold, as had all intercommunicating doors, but the latter have since been replaced. Fortunately, buried beneath successive layers of linoleum, the original wood floors had survived, as had the window shutters.

Despite its great size, the house does not hold very many rooms: just two on the ground floor and three on each of those above. Limited financial resources means the owner has lightly decorated the principal spaces, but he also argues with good reason that their remarkable architectural qualities are best appreciated without the distraction of too much furniture and pictures. The first-floor reception rooms come into their own when lit at night by candles alone. On such an occasion it is possible to imagine the house as it must have been more than 200 years ago when the Earl of Shannon was in residence.

LEFT: At the time of the house's original construction in the early 1730s, its windows would have been much smaller than those seen here; they date from fifty years later when Lord Shannon carried out a program of alterations to bring the building in line with current taste.

FOLLOWING PAGES: Although most of the first floor is taken up by two very large reception rooms, there is also a third space directly above the entrance hall which must once have been a small study or morning room. The present owner has converted it into a kitchen and dining area and, as elsewhere, preserved the evidence of his predecessors' color schemes on the walls.

OPPOSITE: The walls of Pickering Forest's inner hall are covered in prints, reflecting Marina Guinness's particular interest in this art form. "I was going to make a printroom in the house," she jokes, "but then I couldn't afford myself." The antique tricycle was given to her as a child.

TOP RIGHT: In the dining room stands a Chinese lacquered display cabinet in which Marina keeps "my best china—to stop the children from breaking it all." It offers a striking contrast to the woven rush log basket next to the chimneypiece.

BOTTOM RIGHT: One of Pickering Forest's bathrooms. More than forty years ago Marina's late mother, Mariga Guinness, was photographed by Horst for Vogue sitting on the early nineteenth-century sleigh seat.

PICKERING FOREST
COUNTY KILDARE

In 1903 George Brooke, a wealthy wine merchant, Governor of the Bank of Ireland, and cousin of the Brookes of Colebrooke Park, County Fermanagh (one of whom would later become Viscount Alanbrooke, Chief of the Imperial General Staff during the Second World War) was made a baronet.

For the next few years he entertained lavishly at Summerton, the family home on the outskirts of Dublin. So lavishly, in fact, that in 1911 fiscal rectitude required the house be sold and so the Brookes moved permanently to another property they owned in County Kildare called Pickering Forest. Originally this appears to have been two separate small houses used whenever members of the family were hunting in the area and as somewhere to keep their hounds. But in the 1870s, a Brooke had enlarged the building, and in doing so he joined up its disparate parts as well as adding a large drawing room to one side.

Pickering Forest stayed in the Brookes' possession for much of the last century, and they remained devoted to hunting: a report in the Leinster Leader of November 1958 described the inaugural meet of the Kildare Hunt for the season when Sir George Brooke, son of the former Master, the late Sir Francis Brooke, was the new joint-Master. The family was colorful enough to have provided many entertaining stories in the locality. One chatelaine was so untidy she became known as "The Unmade Bed," while another family member, renowned for his chattiness, was nicknamed "The Babbling Brooke." A neighbor, genealogist Harry McDowell, remembers Mabel, Lady Brooke, widow of the second baronet, presiding over grand parties at which the cook's son would be drafted to call out the names of arriving guests. The drawing room suffered from severe damp and, Harry recalls, in the days leading up to any social occasion, "the first objective was to dry out the carpet, and a fire was kept burning night and day while steam gently misted over the eighteenth-century chandelier and mirror glass. When the room filled with people, little droplets of condensation fell unnoticed from the ceiling."

The present owner of the house, Marina Guinness, can testify to the dampness of Pickering Forest when she bought the place in 1990. Daughter of the Hon Desmond Guinness and his late first wife Mariga, she

had grown up not far away in Leixlip Castle and, following the death of her mother, was looking for a house in the area. After acquiring Pickering, she discovered "things were a whole lot worse than I'd thought beforehand. The floorboards, the roof, the wiring: they all had to be replaced. The last family that lived here kept one room warm at the back of the house over the basement—and then they went through the floorboards!"

LEFT, ABOVE, AND OPPOSITE: The library connects the entrance hall with the drawing room. The blue border with gold stars above the paintwork was made by craftsman David Skinner for St Aidan's Cathedral, Enniscorthy, County Wexford. However, when not accepted by the church authorities, Marina Guinness cut the paper into strips and pasted it immediately below the ceiling. The chimneypiece is a replacement for one sold out of the house before she bought it, while the mahogany table decorated with swags originally belonged to her stepmother's mother and aunt, Baby and Zita Jungman; "It had a formica top but I took that off," says Marina.

OPPOSITE AND THIS PAGE: On the dining room walls hang Soviet Russian posters formerly belonging to Zita Jungman; in 1929 she accompanied Lady Cynthia Mosley, Labour Party MP and wife of Sir Oswald Mosley (later to marry Marina's grandmother, Diana Mitford), to visit the exiled Leon Trotsky on the island of Prinkipo, off Istanbul. The mahogany hunting table came from Doneraile Court, County Cork, and the carpet from Shankill Castle, County Kilkenny.

THIS PAGE: Before Marina Guinness bought Pickering Forest, the kitchen was in a wing, but she moved it into the main house and installed a large AGA that provides more heat than had ever been available before. On the wall to the right hang a landscape by John Edwards and an oil of two mackerel by Bea Heather: "I love the fact that they look so miserable," says Marina.

BELOW: The walls of this bedroom are covered in a gold-stamped paper made by David Skinner similar to that once used for wrapping packages. "It's like being inside a parcel," Marina remarks.

RIGHT: Open doors off a bedroom corridor reveal Marina has inherited the same fearless approach to color demonstrated by her parents when they decorated nearby Leixlip Castle.

As befits someone whose parents founded the Irish Georgian Society, Marina takes an entirely pragmatic approach to such problems, observing that "it's cheaper to buy a big house than a small one because nobody wants the big ones," and reporting her father's remark, "nobody ever died from dry rot but a lot of people have contemplated suicide when faced with the cost of eradicating it." Nevertheless, over almost two decades she has undertaken a huge program of restoration which has transformed Pickering into a cozy, if somewhat ramshackle, home for herself and her three children as well as an ever-changing cast of guests. Highly sociable, Marina seems to extend a welcome to almost anyone who arrives on her doorstep but she has a particular partiality for musicians, many of whom have recorded new work at Pickering Forest. "I'm all for encouraging young people," she

"It's cheaper to buy a big house than a small one because nobody wants the big ones."

told a newspaper reporter in July 2008. "Because it doesn't cost anything to rehearse here, we take in people who are interested in doing the work, but don't necessarily have the money to get it done."

Marina has always had a strong interest in music: Stewart Copeland, drummer with The Police, is the father of her elder son Patrick. But she became more actively involved in the business thanks to record producer Denny Cordell, father of her younger son, Finbar. Not long after Cordell's death in 1995, Marina came into contact with the Irish folk band Kila and invited its members to use Pickering Forest as a base for rehearsing and recording. It was the start of what has turned out to be a long and happy association. As one of Kila's members has acknowledged, working at Pickering Forest, "you become part of the family, and that's very conducive to creating—to get you to the stage of producing something. It's so much nicer than a specifically designed studio." Most recently Kila has worked at Pickering on the music for a full-length animated film, The Secret of Kells.

Like its guests, the decoration of Pickering Forest is in a constant state of flux.

Now the house's old drawing room, where Lady Brooke once entertained other remnants of the Anglo-Irish gentry, is filled with musical instruments and recording equipment as many other bands and individuals have discovered its advantages. Glen Hansard and his partner Markéta Irglová, who together won an Oscar for Best Song at the 2008 Academy Awards (for "Falling Slowly" from the film Once), live in a wing of the house and often work there, as do The Frames, Damien Rice, and Fionn Regan among others. "Now it's all spread as far as the library," says Marina. "It's great fun and I'm happy to be of help."

She is more likely to be found in the kitchen than the drawing room, not least because of the former's large stove, making it the warmest place in the house. Decoration here, as elsewhere, is constantly in a state of flux. Although core pieces of furniture, such as those inherited from Mariga Guinness, remain a constant, other items, like her house guests, are more transitory. At one stage Pickering contained 75 chairs that had come from a restaurant but gradually one by one these were taken away by passing friends. "If you're in a big house," Marina remarks, "it can feel empty because people lend you things and then want them back. But then somehow it seems to fill up again."

TOP LEFT: In one of the guest bedrooms, below an unframed landscape canvas sits an early nineteenth-century neo-classical bed decorated with gilt sphinx heads.

TOP RIGHT: Another guest bedroom is dominated by this Chinese bed, believed to have come from an opium den. Seemingly its unusual length was intended to allow two smokers to occupy the one space at the same time.

OPPOSITE: Marina's own four-poster bed was bought by her parents at a house contents sale held in the early 1960s at the vast neo-Gothic Charleville Castle, County Offaly. She says the folds of its original red felted wool curtains have long been home to a small Pipistrelle bat and is untroubled about sharing her rest with this creature.

THIS PAGE: The main staircase at Pickering Forest climbs three storeys. The house was extensively remodeled by a member of the Brooke family after his marriage in 1875, but following the death of his wife in childbirth, he left the house and the family only returned there when they were obliged to sell their principal residence in 1911.

INDEX

Note: Page numbers in bold refer to illustrations and captions

ACKNOWLEDGMENTS

from ROBERT O'BYRNE

I would like to express my sincere thanks to all those house owners whose properties feature in this book, and whose kindness, tolerance, and help during the course of its preparation were very much appreciated. I would also like to express my gratitude to everyone who was nagged and cajoled into suggesting possible properties, as well as to the many owners who allowed me to visit their homes even though, for various reasons, these do not appear in the present work. Perhaps in a second volume...

from SIMON BROWN

I would like to send love and thanks to Liz, Lois, Milo, and Finn Brown; to Philip, Noreen, and Sarah; and to John and Odette Rocha for their help, support, and kindness. Also, I would like to say a big "thank you" to the home owners in this book for their kindness and hospitality and for their vision in making such beautiful and inspirational homes.